I Live in the
Land of Apples

by JoAnna Blaine Easton

ONION
RIVER

PRESS

Burlington, Vermont

Onion River Press
191 Bank Street
Burlington, VT 05401
ISBN: 978-1-949066-27-2 paperback

Printed in the United States of America

Acknowledgements

With heartfelt thanks to those without whose generous
support I may have floundered along the way:

Denise Shekerjian – for our early work together
and her encouragement to publish
Rachel Fisher of Onion River Press – for her guidance on
how to get from manuscript form to book form
Matt Heywood of The Image Farm – for his inspired
cover and interior design work
Rumi and Roxy – my dogs, who lay at my feet
and accompanied me on our long, forays into nature,
which nourished this project

And, most especially, to Christina Koliander –
for her reading and rereading the text and
offering me detailed feedback on everything from
grammar innuendos to content
Her insights and advice have assisted me in
bringing this book to fruition

The cover photograph of me was taken when I was four years old while bravely trying to manage my wild intensity and survive the orphan-like chaos and loneliness of my childhood. There are many dualities in my life, which started early and have shaped my journey. These include growing up in bi-ethnic household; being a twin; being introverted and feisty; being cerebral and emotional; and being reflective and profoundly physical.

I made it and am here to describe the journey. My memories are imperfect, but I am sharing them to the best of my knowledge.

I am a writer, photographer, and poet with a story to tell. The experience of being me sat inside me like a puzzle and, as I arched toward that mystery, I wandered through the labyrinth of experience in a steady search for self-knowledge in order to manage my yen toward mastery and my desire to be loved.

also

The notion of mother – the one who gave me birth, the father who stood in her stead, my hard-earned skill at self-mothering, my surrogate mother, and later, my own mothering of two fabulous daughters – weaves in and around my story.

And I let myself be drawn in…

Let yourself be silently drawn
by the strange pull of what you really love.
It will not lead you astray.

~ Rumi ~

This memoir is dedicated to my father
Samuel Merle Easton
and
to my two beautiful daughters
Amanda and Deva
for life without them, as my greatest gift to the world,
would wither and wilt and die.
I love them beyond all else.

On April 24th, 2009 Mark Robson, a seasoned rescue pilot, waited for his plane at the small airport near Fort Lauderdale, Florida. By fate or coincidence, I too was in that tiny, unremarkable room on my way to Cat Cay where my beloved brother, Ed, hosts our annual nuclear family reunion. Though these reunions are motivated by the best of intentions, the gatherings can be regressive: eight children and my inadequate mother, face-to-face for a weekend of bridge, ocean, food and more than a few tense exchanges.

The pilot and I were drawn together across the small waiting room. "It's Poets' Day," he announced joyfully and recited from memory Mary Oliver's "A Dream of Trees." It is one of my favorites, and he followed it with three Plato quotes, also from memory, about the relationship between retreating and death so tenderly referenced in the Oliver poem. He was a gift, a kindred soul, and we spoke for the hour we had together about all that is held in this remarkable poem and more.

As we exchanged background information, I learned that Mark had worked for 16 years for the United Nations on refugee recovery missions in 47 countries, many of these at war. Of late, he was volunteering his flight skills to train other rescue pilots. It turned out that the Irish had spit in his blood too. We shared that cultural connection, our love of poetry and discourse, and exchanged an astonishing amount of philosophy in a brief amount of time. I couldn't have had this conversation with anyone in my family. It was one of those rare encounters: unexpected, quick, deep, and filled with lasting meaning.

As our flight was called, Mark walked me over to my family now gathered in a circle. I see us moving in their direction, and I feel the fullness of our exchange trailing behind us like a plump balloon full of wonder. I am overcome with the knowledge that my inner life, full of poetry and philosophy and shared with this complete stranger has rarely, if ever, been visible to the people in this family-circle.

Mark greeted everyone politely including my mother, who waved her trembling, liver-spotted hand around the circle and bragged about being here with her eight children for a reunion.

"Oh," he said, "Eight children! There is an Irish legend about the mystical and perceptive qualities of the seventh born. Seven is a magical number. It is a powerful, lucky number, and the seventh child is said to possess the psychic powers to decode secrets and reveal inner truths. Who is your seventh child?" he asked.

"He is," my mother answered as she beamed toward my twin brother, Joe. "Joe has all of those qualities."

"No Mother, I am the seventh child," I interjected. How like her to deny me this small measure of respect and appreciation.

Mark, his eyes on me, nodded thoughtfully. "Yes, it must be her; I can see it so clearly."

Silence. Not even a nod or smile from my mother or the others. And then he was off.

My journal entry the following day captures my reflections: *I know pain comes when pain is a teacher. And, I know rescue pilots come when rescue pilots are needed. Maybe in some unknown way, this experience will alter my fate in ways I cannot foresee right now. Did anyone catch the meaning of this "show down" besides me and Mark? No one saw my spirit glow in Mark's sunshine and collapse around the draining sinkhole called mother. I am nearly invisible to my family.*

In that same entry, I went on to map out my plan to write this story. The pilot was gone – in my life a mere hour – but his message, and the depth of knowledge he acquired of me so quickly endure and are forever entangled with the wisdom of Mary Oliver and Plato and the legend of the seventh child. The final three-line refrain from that magical poem inform this story, a memoir:

> *The blades of every crisis point the way.*
> *I would it were not so but so it is*
> *Who ever made music of a mild day?*

> *Mary Oliver*

> ...

Motherless children bear an indelible mark of loneliness and longing. For these children, something substantial goes missing at an early age, and the black hole informs many of the life choices that follow. Some don't make it without this essential veil of love and protection; others, like myself, find ways to compensate and develop potent narratives to take the sting off the wound. Bandaids and narratives abound in my life and, I suspect, in the lives of those who are or feel motherless all over the world. We are survivors.

After my encounter with the rescue pilot, I was intrigued to learn that the archetype of the seventh-born child bears its own mystique. It appears in myths and folktales in many countries from Ireland to Iberia. The number seven itself is prevalent in uncanny ways: seven continents, seven chakras, seven days of the week, seven colors of the rainbow. Professor Vaz da Silva, a European Studies scholar, examined ethnography and folklore to explain the dangers and mysteries of the seventh born child. According to these myths, he contends, the seventh child stands apart from the family as it breaks the double trinity of the six children before it. This child is often neglected as it is deemed in excess of parent capacity, which adds social stigma as well. The exceptionality of this seventh child is associated with both mysticism and witchcraft in folklore. A less academic yet enchanting story of a seventh daughter is told by folklorist writer, Juliet Marillier, in *Daughter of the Forest.* I read this chubby novel subsequent to my encounter with rescue pilot Mark and fell in love with the lovely Sorcha, a seventh child who grows up half-wild in the forest of Sevenwaters; she is guided by the luck of Fair Folk to develop her healing powers. Having the capacity to heal is also prevalent in the seventh born child.

My earliest response to the conditions of my life begin in Rosealia Hospital, in Pittsburgh, Pennsylvania on December 3rd, 1949 at 6:35 p.m. This is the place, date, and time of my birth. My twin brother, Joseph Wayne Easton, "had been a gentleman and let you out first," my mother boasted on his behalf early and often though she forgot this fact when putting Joe on a pedestal at the airport. I weighed 6 pounds 10 ounces at birth; Joe was underweight and had to be in an incubator. I got the lion's share which, within the first breath of life, cast me as wolfish in my mother's eyes, sealing my fate in countless ways. My mother was fully anesthetized for our birth, customary for some mothers in her generation in America. Within minutes of my birth, I was separated from my mother and my fraternal twin.

As the story goes, my mother awoke at dawn to the voice of a nun, the baker working at Roselia Hospital. The nun was running through the maternity ward questioning, "Who birthed those twins?" Once she learned it was my mother, she said, "Those are very special children. They will do great work in the vineyard of Christ." Ostensibly, this nun died within a few days of this announcement making her message especially auspicious. Though I find the Catholic, biblical imagery suspect, it fit the bill for my mother adding a mystical dimension to our birth story.

My mother went home to her other six children for Christmas and returned to pick us up sometime afterwards, 22 or 28 days later, though the actual date is unknown. She claims, in her defense, that her doctor recommended this idea to her and, in those days, doctors were treated like God, but it also belies her lack of will and instinct. While home, a woman named Leona was hired to take care of *the twins* as my mother was apparently overwhelmed. Leona was a heavy set spinster with dozens of moles and wire-rim glasses on her face, based on early photographs of her holding us. My mother did not breast feed any of her children, whether typical of her day or specific to her character – who knows? To be able to afford formula was a status symbol of wealth and may have appealed to my mother. If held at all, I was held by nuns for the first three weeks of my life, often not the most maternal of women, and later by a spinster nanny, hardly an ideal birth and bonding experience.

Rosealia

My mother was drugged
and in the hands of her doctor,
who had delivered her last six babies,
advised gallstone surgery, and
discouraged her from bearing the burden
of taking us home. He claimed to know
her thin life might crack open.

Maybe he was right as
he had seen the black and blues
on the side of her sagging breasts
inside her pale thighs,
and this same man delivered us
into the unschooled arms of nuns
sending our mother home
to her other six children.

Gorgeous new twins
in a hospital with a pretty name:
Rosealia – much prettier
than having no one
trace with wonder
the miniature tulips
on our baby blankets.

مزرعة التفاح

More than a half mile above sea level in the Zgharta district, Mazraat el Toufah or *The Land of Apples* floats in the mountains of Lebanon and is home to my father's family. I have lived there always and live there now more than ever, though never literally. The full knowledge and acceptance of this has been building in me just as this story, this memoir, has emerged organically from the debris and compost laid down and layered by years of dreams and life happenings.

My father, Samuel Merle Easton (1906-1999) was Lebanese, and it is his ethnicity, food, warmth and amber-eyed vision that cradled me. I am his child. Generous and hot tempered, he was often loud and aggressive toward my mother, who tortured him with her haughtiness, provocations, and withholding. He often turned his anger toward my mother and occasionally toward the other seven, but never toward me. In my own way, I understood the sadness beneath his anger and chose to steer clear of the topical gusts of temper. At his request, I mated socks and shoved quarters into cardboard sleeves. I polished his shoes and was his sous chef. I made sacrifices to please him as I enjoyed his company when he was happy and satisfied. Memories of him come alive when I smell caramelized onion and garlic, cigar smoke, or the tallow-turpentine-waxy smell of shoe polish. I treasure the hours I spent at his side peeling onions, chopping peppers, and learning to squeeze and smell fruit and vegetables to judge their ripeness and readiness. Standing on a stool next to him by the stove to dunk a crust of bread in the simmering tomato sauce we made together remains a peak memory of experiences we shared. The daddy-jobs I performed with socks, quarters, and shoes were tasks with disorderly beginnings and satisfying endings. I cut my teeth on mastery at this level and later tried my hand at more demanding undertakings.

My inherited blend of love and anger, temper and force have reared up many times in my life, but I have no misgivings about my zigzag growth pattern, nor about the disdain I feel toward my mother and depth of love I feel for my father. Though I believe that soul, spirit, the stars and past lives enhance our gene pool in mysterious ways, and I am in awe of those mysteries, I want to believe that the *mother load* of my genetic wiring comes mostly from my father. The rewards of being his daughter far outweigh the shadows. It is the residue of his light in me that informs how I cook, parent my daughters, love my dogs, and live my womanhood.

Perhaps the most fruitful and formative response I had in early life was a sharp emotional turn away from my mother and toward my father. My father is to my mind my mother and, given the options and that this turn was made so early in life, it came more from the heart than the mind: I made an excellent choice. In spirit, I live in the land of apples with my father and his kin. Still, he was an imperfect man, hindered by his lack of education and his marriage, the latter of which would have killed a lesser man. Instead, the challenges of his sexual frustration and emasculating wife often were expressed as anger and, yes, he beat my mother often in his fits of rage. I wrote this poem below at the same place and time that I took the portrait photograph of my father in 1992; he was in his 80s.

Mangroves

In a fierce afternoon heat
my father sits wise and terrible
his stoned-faced presence
inaudible as stars,
a wizard in the shade
of stringy mangrove and
Spanish moss.

He will be eighty-six in June
he looks but sees nothing
beyond his interior.
He has become remote;
his hands lay childlike in his lap
no longer flexed fists
on leg-sized arms
poised to strike my mother.

Today, I hear and see a coolness
of a heat no longer white with rage –
if still unspent, it has melted
like clouds into rain.

My hands twitch then move
with something like forgiveness
and cover my father's folded hands.

He registers my love in silence.
Wet and fallen leaves layer
under his wrought-iron weight.

Lebanon is often referred to as the "Pearl of the Middle East." It is the only Middle Eastern country with no desert while it spans about 4000 miles. According to Bob Joseph, an historian on Lebanon, Lebanese people are not Arab; they are decedents of the Phoenicians. Lebanon is a parliamentary democratic republic with notable respect for public liberties, and its constitution protects the dignity of various religions and sects. Forty percent of the inhabitants of Lebanon are Catholic. Mazraat El Toufah (MET) is a small town in the mountains opposite of Jerusalem about one hour North of Tripoli.

Mazraat El Toufah means apple garden or land or apples. There is a French, Maronite Catholic convent outside of MET where the Catholic rituals are performed in Aramatic, the same language Jesus purportedly spoke. History tells that the Ottomans came to convert the populace to Islam, which caused the Catholics to flee into the mountains. Monasteries, caves, apple orchards, churches, mountain views and the town itself are at cloud level. Mountain tops have religious significance for biblical cultures and sages of all wisdom traditions, for it is said that the spirit reveals itself in those lofty places.

While in Mazraat el Toufah only briefly, my nephew, Mac, visited the church and graveyard where my father's grandfather and his great Uncle, Salim, are buried. Salim is perhaps the inspiration for my father's name, Samuel. Ostensibly, this graveyard is located only ten feet from the spot where Abraham was ordered to sacrifice his son, Isaac, in the mountainous region of Moriah. Though at first standoffish, the 104-year-old, unknown relative welled with tears when he realized how Mac and he were related. He told story after story including how one family member had found a pot of gold and performed a miracle. These are regional stories and, understandably, the bible is taken quite literally in a region that is virtually the setting of nearly all biblical stories. In any event, my father's family was loved and revered, and Mac felt like the prodigal son during his short visit. My father attempted to return several times before his death, but the borders kept closing and his plans never came to fruition. Though my father lived a charmed life, this was one of his dreams that went unfulfilled. I guess it is a rare person who dies having done everything they hoped to do, but that my father was unable to go to Mazraat el Toufah and stand next to that church and those graves and hold the wrinkled hands of his relatives was a great loss to him and to all of us, for he would have woven himself and us back into the land of apples.

While structuring and writing this memoir, trying to dream my way into its center, it became clear to me that apple trees and the twisting shapes of olive trees figure large in my history. Perhaps they look alike because their fruit is valued as a commodity, so they are likely planted, grafted and pruned similarly. We begin here in the shade of the apple tree to the side and back of my childhood home south of Pittsburgh. If I close my eyes, I can see the yellow-green leaves of spring mutate into a blue-green in summer and become a bed of rusty-green leaves in fall. I dreamed often under that tree and those dreams followed the sinewy branches, leaves and fruit. An essential belonging got writ into my psyche in its shadow. Tasting apples and inhaling the leafy-mud smell after a rain still brings on a swoon. Blackish branches bejeweled with half-frozen, golden apples in winter reigns as my quintessential Christmas tree. I hung upside down by my knees, climbed higher than I should have, played mumbly peg with a switchblade and caught lightning bugs on the cool earth in the shade around its trunk. When the lowest branch was sawed off, I dried off the sweet seepage with my shirt and patched its wound with dirt and spit. With no other tools at hand, I engaged my nurturing heart. I spent more hours under that apple tree than in my bed.

Olive trees came later in my life as did a taste for olives. When living in Europe in my twenties, I visited Italy often by train and went down to stay with my first boyfriend, Stephen, on Crete. This visit lasted six months and though fishing by night with lanterns stirred my imagination, the fresh sheep cheese, tomatoes and olives grabbed my heart. The olive groves, farmers and the pressing of olive oil intrigued me. I am more an earth baby than a water baby so, in Greece, I volunteered my services in olive groves just to sweat and be next to the trees and the workers. Both Italy and Greece boast an affection for olives and the production and exportation of olive oil is big business. Additionally, both Italian and Greek cuisine have the Mediterranean flare and flavor I know and love. Later in life, I saw olive groves in paintings by my surrogate mother, Frau Engels, who visited and painted in Greece annually. My favorite one hangs in my bedroom, a gift from her. Greece was her second home and became mine by association.

Something about the Y-shape opening of the branches and the blackish bark draws me in and feels inexplicably familiar. I had a repetitive pre-adolescent dream where the Y in a tree played a significant role. Apples are in the Rosaceae family and olives in the Oleaceae family. I have just looked that up. One is sweet and the other, bitter, peppery and inedible until cured. Both are essential fruits, one the bedrock of dessert dishes while the other is savory, and each make my mouth water when I think of them. To my eye, the trees themselves bear resemblance to each other, especially the old trees, and stir the beauty response in me.

Apples are equated with the human desire for sweetness. English poet, Matthew Arnold and satirist, Jonathan Swift, called their highest ideals "sweetness and light." Food writer Michael Pollan describes four human desires and associates them with specific plants in his unforgettable inquiry called *The Botany of Desire*. His thesis, in brief, states that human desire has driven the cultivation and preservation of certain plants because humans seek: sweetness, beauty, intoxication and control. Perhaps my psyche knew that I would have to seek and receive sweetness in things or food, not in my mother to be sure. Pollan, in discussing the apple, outlines the co-evolution that occurred between plants and animals. The apple offered sweet flesh to satisfy the mammalian sweet tooth, but only once the poison tainted seed inside had matured completely. The animals offered transportation to the seeds, so the plant had a chance to grow in a wide variety of climates. From Michael Pollan: *Like Dionysus, John Chapman was an agent of domestication. With every cider orchard he helped plant, the wilderness became that much more hospitable and homelike.* When I read this, so many things converged in me. Johnny Appleseed went around seeding the New World with apples, and the product of his wanderings brought civility to the wilderness along with sweetness and intoxication (fermented cider) to people. For me the apple is home plate. As a child, I wandered around the vast unpopulated acres for hours and came home at dusk to the apple tree, not the living room. I lived in the land of apples in this way too.

Being from a large family of eight and the seventh child has its benefits and horrors. Often I felt that ours was a household with no adults, and though I look back on this with fear sometimes, I also know it gave me the freedom to be my own authority and shape my thinking based on experience. On the horror side of things, I could be gone for four or five hours and no one seemed to know I was missing. There were no search parties and no admonitions or questions upon my return. I slipped through the veil – from family to my interior world of open fields and back to family with no restrictions or explanations needed. I also played with sharp tools, rusty buckets, and switchblades long before I understood the dangers and no adult intervened. The benefits were many: freedom, independence, self reliance and the games of Monopoly, poker and especially Mumbly Peg among them. The down side? It felt like no one had my back. A kind of wild and orphaned look shows up often in early photographs of me.

In order to explain the game, I just looked Mumbly Peg up in the Encyclopedia Britannica where it is described as follows: *Mumblety-peg, also spelled mumbledy-peg, or mumbly-peg, original name mumble the peg, is a game of skill played with a knife, usually a jackknife. The game was played as early as the 17th century in the British Isles. The object of the game is for each player to flip or toss the knife in a progression of moves such that, after each one, the knife sticks in the ground and stands erect. Although positions vary, the most common ones are (1) flipping from the palm, (2) flipping from the back of the hand, (3) flipping by a twist of the fist, (4) throwing by holding the blade tip between the thumb and forefinger, (5) flipping from between the teeth, (6) throwing from each shoulder or behind each ear, (7) tossing backward over the head, and (8) throwing around the head from the back.*

Mumbly Peg

There were eight of us at dusk
under the apple tree
seated on numb legs
on the shadows of spiny branches
waiting to charm the knife
onyx-handled in the black light.

My turn to cradle
and charge the knife
release it, flip it
blade icy on my fingertips;
flick it crisp from the forehead
nose, chin, shoulder
elbow and wrist, then
mark my dirty knee.

Finally, after years of
play and practice,
I turn to the darkness
and face the apple tree
the knife in its hand bed.

Now call in all the powers
flip it up over my curly head
listen for the silent somersault
of heart and blade,
listen for the earth to slice open
for the black quartz to quiver
for the blade to vibrate into song.

This poem "Mumbly Peg," written in my first poetry writing class with John Engels and Alan Broughton some 20 years ago, brings back one of those ecstatically rich, dark and erotic experiences, reminding me of how early my yen for mastery was engaged. This is a curious theme in my life, which I now see as springing up from some well inside me: a trademark. We began the writing class with the assignment of writing a 50 page autobiography in the third person. The idea was to mine that material for poetic or short story material depending on which direction you went. After that first assignment, we were divided into two sections of our choice: short story or poetry. I chose poetry. Mastery, motherlessness and fate were themes that arose in that early effort and are still hauntingly present. No doubt, my childhood rattled my nerves and often I felt at sea and without viable role models. Perhaps the depth of immersion and the steadying effects of practice required for mastery were in response to my need for a sense of order and perfection. These things I mastered were tangible measuring sticks; they stood still, unlike a person, and as I grew in skill measurably, I grew in confidence and self love. Games, I now see, were opportunities for childhood mastery and the material I used to layer and merge aesthetics, nature, memory and even olive and apple trees, which came later. Having no mother is difficult, having a bad mother is in some ways maybe harder because she is there physically, but she does not participate in the tender act of mothering. Many of my hour-long escapes away from home took me to Pop Shram's, a recreation business now defunct.

POP SHRAM'S PLACE

Way down there, through the brambly hillside
Behind old man Chew's boarded-up place
Rushing across the splintery bridge, barefoot
and shirtless still, at eleven, in July,
I arrived at Pop Shram's hot and thirsty.

I dug out a pile of Indian head nickels
from my pocket,
drank green lemonade,
strung and handled the bow,
fastened my hand
around its buttery, leather grip
in a handshake with a friend.

Focused with tense desire
on the bull's eye,
at a makeshift target
wired over lumpy wild straw.
A concentric blur of blues and whites
spiraled in toward the center
and pulled me in with them.

A swirl of hair
stood and danced
at the base of my neck
electric in the sunlight,
and I took final aim
whoosh, hiss, thunk
a bull's eye.

In that same writing class, my teachers especially admired the "special energy and urgency" in my poem 'Apple Orchard," which takes place in a Vermont apple orchard with my daughters, where I experienced a state of mystical union with them, the light, and the trees. This experience, the poem and the photographs of my daughters in that moment, reveal what anchors my steady exploration of the power of eros, internally and externally through words and images.

Apple Orchard

Hundreds of deep-split blackened-bark apple trees
in full faded-pink bloom rushing
down the hillside to the lake.
I veered, swayed into them –
down deeply into
those Grecian olivey-apple trees
split wide open.

The children wandered in – disturbing nothing.
They walked in and belonged.
Their arms out – their iridescence meeting –
still green and early –
both the blossoms and the children
on spiny branches, on olivey-apple trees.

All three of these poems originate from the imprint of early experiences, which reveal a capacity for eros and mystical experience. I speak of love and mysticism not in a particularly sexual or religious way, but as a divine force or a current that carried me. I had and have a penchant for participating in life with my senses alive and my life force engaged in whatever I am drawn into at the time. I understood, often sought, and received *energy medicine.* The buttery sheets in my crib and the sound of the switchblade as it sliced into the earth engaged my tactile and sensuous nature. I came into the world this way and have learned to honor it. Being outside as a child was where I came alive and, in those many hours alone, I was keenly observant and reverent. Maybe it is unusual to move into stillness as a response to arousal, I don't know, but I know it was my way and that magic happens for me in this twilight state. There exists a photo of me still in diapers in full mediation, arms out and eyes closed, which illustrates some unknown and early draw to spirit; maybe that nun in the hospital who remarked on the character of the twins the day we were born was right – I am a creature infused with the mystical.

My dad's mother, Nagibi Wakim left Lebanon and then France on a ship named La Gascogne from Havre, France in 1901. She was 14 years old and sailed with her sister, Latifie, who was 15 years old; they listed their mother and Pittsburgh as their destination. In my childhood, she and her children came to our house once a month on Sundays to eat Kibbe and Syrian rice, drink strong coffee and smoke cedary-cigars. They spoke Lebanese while I sat on the edge of our mandala designed rugs, at the feet of our matriarch in the stupor of language-music and cigar smoke. My grandfather, Marone Gustine (or Augustine or Yustein), was no longer alive when my memories begin though I do remember being forced to kiss his icy hands as he lay in the coffin as a sign of respect and love. I leaned in fright over the coffin anchored in the arms of my father, who whispered, "It's alright, honey. Give his hands a kiss; it's a sign of respect." When immigrating, our last name was changed to Easton; it meant from the east and supposedly held some of the sound of our original name. I didn't glean many facts on those ancestral Sundays, but for those hours I was transported to the land of apples with my Lebanese clan and learned how to be part of Lebanese culture: more games, eros and mysticism.

GameDances

The room reeled with steamy-coffee
and cedary-smoke from Cuban cigars,
where Nagibi and her five sons –
my audience – squatted floor level
on the rim of a Lebanese carpet universe.

Inside the black and scarlet borders,
I twirled in the maze of genetic geometry.
The mandala-middle mesmerizing me,
when, out of the dark half of a child's life,
grew the hypnosis of my gamedances.

Moving so deep – and so entwined with
the smokey-thick and intoxicating music
of a swaying, lilting-liturgy of Arabic words,
my feet hit the electric blues, reds and blacks
in staccato flits and flutters.

Pulled in, under and around colorful corners,
in breathless and happy circles
to my heart-beating ancestral drum
in the midst of iconic-loving faces,
I danced myself real.

I did what I called "gamedances" in the sacred geometry of the Lebanese carpets and on Carrara marble floor tile with red grout on the kitchen floor. I call my play "gamedances" in part because my movements had a game quality in that I moved across the floor like one would on a game board as in Monopoly or Sorry. It also harkened to dance as I fell into a kind of trance, and I wanted my movements to entertain my Lebanese elders and to have enough grace and surprise to please my audience. According to those who study sacred geometry, it draws on mathematical principles and the shapes and patterns in shells and other natural forms. The chambered nautilus is a prime example as, according to Australian author, Dr. Stephen Skinner: *it grows at a constant rate and so its shell forms a logarithmic spiral to accommodate that growth without changing shape. Also, honeybees construct hexagonal cells to hold their honey.* Tabernacles, mosques and altars are often designed and constructed around these same principles. Certain religions prohibit the use of humans or animals as their sacred objects thus the mandala was favored as a central medallion. As I moved on our rugs, I felt like I was magnetically participating in the physical, magnetic pull of sacred geometry.

The color red united many special features of my childhood. Red is an emotionally intense color. It's the color of blood and apples and the saris of Indian and Nepali married women. Blood flows and oozes, brings life and bodes death. Red is passion and the color of fire; it expresses power and love as in the robes of kings. It is said to enhance human metabolism. My father's input, choice of colors, the type of layout and stone used, and the wood chosen created the interior and exterior of our home, which he had built around his aesthetics. There was a distinctly un-American feel to the inside of our house. We did not have wall-to-wall carpeting nor any plastic or cheap furnishings.

The dining room set was mahogany and our dishes were old-fashioned in design and color: brown and white. The den was paneled in knotty pine, and we had thick blocks of opaque glass around the front door, which distorted light and images from the outside. I spent time in each of these rooms, traced the knots in the pine with my fingers and squinted at the light bending through the glass and slatted blinds. What I saw on a daily basis was not that which my friends at school saw in their homes.

The union of light and form, nature and me, has launched countless musings, questions and insights, which are imprinted in me like watermarks on paper. From early on, I knew the tingling and explosive power of being at the intersection of fierce energetic connections. The almost magnetic pull of these experiences gave way to an understanding that I had some magnetic force in me. My inner world often would both light up and become still at the sight of a certain something and transcendent moments ensued. My earliest memory of this is watching dust moats dancing through the slats of Venetian blinds while running my hands on the creamy softness of my crib sheets. I later thought about this as a "body-of-light" kind of moment. I also have early memories of crying in my crib and no one coming to check in on me or pick me up. Was it neglect or apathy? I would tuck my knees up into the yogic child's pose and rock myself back to sleep. My mother concluded, in conversation with that same doctor who encouraged her desire to leave us in the hospital, I was "oversexed." What an odd conclusion. How about tiredness or fright? Not surprisingly, it never occurred to her that maybe this baby, me, was asking to be picked up, cuddled and nestled, held and rocked against a warm, loving *motherbody*. My mother lacked the capacity to love or to know certain things that I knew and felt as a baby. I lost respect for her early on and never regained it.

Left to my own devices, or perhaps by nature and lack of nurture, I developed a rich, quasi-mystical, quasi-spiritual life. When these union experience happen, a high-pitched, sensuous input of sight, movement and touch causes time to pause and then stand still and brings with it the space in which a nonverbal insight or a "knowing" occurs. Usually I "think" in words and sentences and arrive at an understanding that way. The nonverbal insight stands out as a different path to understanding, more related to the way an ephipany or knowing something with your gut occurs. In high school, for example, I became a nationally ranked gymnast, and I remember a very similar state of mind rising out of my pinpoint concentration. I could foresee the next move on the balance beam and focus my body and my senses into a laser sharp execution of the aerial back walkover or dismount. Love and concentration contributed to my journey toward mastery of the many interests I pursued throughout my life: childhood games, gymnastics, sewing, gardening, writing, biking, yoga, cooking and baking, photography and academic endeavors.

The sharpest of these union experiences occurred when I was 26 years-old standing on the steps leading to the Van Hise building on the University of Wisconsin, Madison campus. It was accompanied by what I think of as the *music of the spheres*. This was not music you could hear per se, but refers to a spatial relationship among the sun, moon and planets in an alignment said to create an orbital resonance. In my memory of the experience, I saw everything move and pulse to an indescribably sweet and harmonized tempo. My eyes were fixed on a wall of ivy just blushing red in October, and I could feel a kind of exquisite order and harmony to things – temporal and heavenly. The nonverbal insight or experience defies words, in some way, but what I felt was the connecting energy, on a practically atomic level, of all matter: me, the trees, the movement of the people on the green, the clouds in the sky. Synchronicity, maybe? I seek this poem by Rumi, my primary muse for decades and my dog's namesake, when I try to find company in the aftermath of these esoteric experiences.

Spring overall. But inside us
there's another unity.
Behind each eye here,
one glowing water.
Every forest branch moves differently
in the breeze, but as they sway,
they connect at the roots.

Jalāl ad-Dīn Muhammad Rūmī
جلال‌الدين محمد رومى

Where are the roots for a motherless child? I was looking for my connection to the world. At this time in my life, I had returned from having lived in Austria and was reading mostly German philosophers and poets. In this good company, I sought Carl Jung's Eranos lecture (1951), where he offered a full explanation of acausal connectivity and parallelism. Jung used acausal connectivity and synchronicity as synonyms. He defined the experience as *the coming together of inner and outer events in a way that cannot be explained by cause and effect and that is meaningful to the observer.* Coincidence and synchronicity were also explored by many physicists and psychiatrists. I made some sense out of my experiences through reading and studying. But it was my Jungian analyst who gave me concepts and language; she described me as having *mystical intelligence.*

This rush of experience with its corresponding depth was not always a welcome guest though it brought with it a vague sense of transparency, like something sweet moving through me. First, I didn't understand the origin or the purpose of these revelations for many years. Sometimes I didn't want them and couldn't harness or use the otherworldliness transmitted to me. I felt afraid and they contributed to my sense of loneliness and "otherness" as I did not see these qualities in my siblings or friends. Only after many years of such repetitive experiences did I begin to see a pattern, trust the content, and transform these realizations into artistic expression.

My first collection of poems was titled: *The Curse, The Blessing and The Twilight.* Nine poems from this collection were submitted in September, 2008 to Vermont Studio Center, and I was awarded a full fellowship on the basis of this collection. The title of my second collection was *Eros.* Selections from this collection won me entry into the Bread Loaf Writers' Conference. The shift from mistrusting and questioning to naming and valuing is reflected in my poetry from first title to second. As a photographer, I also experimented with capturing these ephemeral experiences in abstract ice, landscapes, and even in portrait work if I saw a kindred spirit aloft.

Still, questions needed answers and so my life as a seeker amped up a notch. Decades of reading and studying, Jungian analysis, art therapy, spiritual study and practice, energy work and metaphorical therapy exercises gave me the tools to unlock mysteries and construct a framework of language and a context of safety within which to open myself to a deeper understanding and appreciation of these meaningful coincidences. Such inquiries enabled me to connect with the knowledge I already had in a conscious way and reflect on how I knew what I know: becoming meta. Seeking answers and balm on the original wound of feeling *unmothered* drove me to esoteric and paranormal sources. Ultimately, my ten year study of yoga with Yogarupa Rod Stryker and other esteemed teachers, culminating in my yoga teacher training license, served to put it all together. Descriptors like mystical intelligence, creative imaginings, peak experience, kinesthesia, microcosmic orbit, synergy, giftedness, tantric union, and artistic disposition lent me the necessary "filing cabinet" in which to hold, examine and value these precocious and persistent happenings.

In 2004, using an *Emergent Knowledge* technique, I created an intimate odyssey on a spatial time line led by a phenomenal psychiatrist. *Emergent Knowledge* is a guided psychological technique developed by the late New Zealand therapist, David Grove. Though guided, it is a process which taps into a person's intuition as the primary guide, absent of influence or interpretation by the therapist. The goal is the discovery of new self knowledge and healing through a process of re-imprinting. Dr. Robert Balaban, my psychiatrist guide, asked me to try to separate my fear of vulnerability and smallness on the one hand from my humming fullness on the other hand. I was asked to pick colors, which would represent my vibrant self; I chose iridescent Byzantine coppery-green and coral. In a meditative state with my eyes closed, I was asked to create images of these two dimensions of self. On my left, I saw an infant, so still, so pale, so nearly dead. On my right, this excitedly fluttering, iridescent green hummingbird with a coral chest. In a subliminal process aimed at integration, the hummingbird flew over and vibrated its wings and its bright coral chest over the infant until she began to move and awaken into life. I *rebirthed* myself with nearly shattering intensity.

There were many such sessions, which worked to bring forward a profoundly early remembrance of helplessness and, equally early, a drive and will to thrive. We moved up through time in this state of remembrance. The final exercise was to create a map on a timeline. I was asked to draw pictures of all major, imprinting events of my life in order to see how each event was part of my personal cosmology. As there are historical narratives attached to each event, I was invited to put phrases with each image. This timeline began just before birth, hence the nearly dead infant. In moving through my life in this way, I was able to create a new core statement about myself.

My timeline was first a series of drawings spanning several pages, which I later taped together into my *Rosetta Stone*. It works like a good Mapquest inquiry and has become the literal map that, once assembled, has lent context to those experiences. In that process, guided by my intuition, I realized definitively that these experiences, 28 separate ones documented from 1949-2004, are mine and reveal my personal cosmology. Like tacking points, certain experiences turn the ship this way and then that. This guided therapy helped explain my 'beingness" to me and possibly my purpose in the world. Though I don't pretend to understand the mystery of existence, still the idea of preordained purpose haunts me. My yoga studies led me to an initiation into a Hindu lineage solidifying my belief in something beyond myself and the surface existence I perceive. Perhaps if I keep mapping the last 14 years and beyond, new revelations would appear that may shed light on the eternal questions that hover over me, my feeling of being *in* this world not *of* this world.

Eros means love or desire in Greek. It also can be associated with the Chinese medicine concept of Qi or life force. I think of love energy as the core of life force: it's my religion. While in middle school and high school, in an effort to channel and express my sometimes volcanic life force, I poured myself into reading, gymnastics, journaling and sewing. From the day I stepped into the hallways of school, I couldn't get enough. My childhood was excessively free from any structured learning and supervision, which I can now see as having been fertile ground for me. Yet, the thirst for learning and experience went unquenched and some of my intellectual curiosity got tangled up in my abundant physical energy. Over time, my capacity for intellectual absorption found a place in my academic and spiritual studies and, consequently, some of my energy got distributed beyond the purely physical.

I was not particularly boy-crazy or interested in dating in high school, maybe because of introversion or, as likely an explanation, I was a geek. The few crushes I had went unreciprocated, though my sister, Pat, up ahead of me two years in high school, reminds me of all the guys who had a crush on me. I try to modify my experience accordingly, but I was a lonely teenager, a serious student, sewing and reading into the midnight hours. Much of my physical energy was channeled into gymnastics, in particular my specialties: vaulting and the balance beam. When I was practicing and competing, an aura of silence enveloped me and the beam: there was nothing else on my radar. Fully absorbed and focused, like cradling the knife for mumbly peg, I had perfect control of my body in space. Each move was part of a dance, precise and mesmerizing to me and to the sparse audience, which rarely if ever included a family member.

In 10th grade English, one day after school, I asked my teacher, Ms. Sandra Kauper, to recommend a book she loved to me. Henry James' *The Portrait of a Lady* shifted my sense of Americans and selfhood. Isabel Archer, the naive and arduous young American, leaves to go live in England, marries there and gets duped by falling into a web of intrigue. She matures, becomes a woman, develops her voice, and transforms herself through experience. As a character, Isabel had a sense of expectancy driven by an internal desire to change; James describes her arching toward an unknown future in this way: *She was restless, and even excited; at moments she trembled a little. She felt that something had happened to her of which the importance was out of proportion to its appearance; there had really been a change in her life. What it would bring with it was as yet extremely indefinite; but Isabel was in a situation which gave a value to any change. She had a desire to leave the past behind her, and, as she said to herself, to begin afresh. This desire, indeed, was not a birth of the present occasion; it was as familiar as the sound of the rain upon the window, and it had led to her beginning afresh a great many times.*

Simultaneously, as co-captain of my high school gymnastics team, I practiced daily and specialized on the balance beam and vaulting. Later that next year, I performed in Nationals and got ranked. In between the reading of that novel and my heart-stilling performance, I understood how I was and was not typically American. The daughter of a Lebanese immigrant father and a Black-Irish, second generation mother, I now registered just how different my home life, the food, the rugs, the energy, and I had always been.

This is how I view my parents and siblings. We grew up in a bi-ethnic household where the seam between one culture and another was not nicely sewn, forcing us to choose. As my parents cultural conflict was writ large, and my mother took a haughty and divisive stance, we were shoved to one side of the fence or the other. This is particularly true for the five youngest in the family and, though adult integration can happen, this has not been true for us. The divide between siblings Sam and Ed has worsened over the years, and I have grown no closer to my mother. My older sisters, Peggy and Jane have a tense relationship. My twin Joe and I have been estranged and rarely speak to each other except when we find ourselves at a family wedding or reunion. Early imprinting is hard to recover from on a micro and macro scale. If post-colonialism and prevalent self-hatred among people who were meant to feel inferior by racial divides is any indication, then it is just as difficult to forget when family ties are built around racism, competition and superiority. I appreciate the effort to reconcile and have made one from time to time, but it has been challenging. Needless to say, this has to do with whether the oppressor evolves or, if there is little to no evolution, then it is particularly hard to want to reconcile. Boundaries to avoid toxic people are also important. Sadly, years later in the throes of post-divorce ugliness, I demonized my ex-husband, not along racial/ethnic lines but rather character lines, but still, I regret this and the effect it has had on my daughters. Pushing children to chose one parent over the other is an ugly game in which everyone loses. This has been a hard-earned realization as, because I chose my father over my mother, perhaps I expected the same of my children. This was unfair and unwise of me; children don't want to split themselves in half. I should have been more aware of this earlier on.

My twin brother and I have quite different energy, interests and values. As kids we played a lot of poker for money, again, my father's influence. He thought poker taught kids math or at least how to count, how to compete in a healthy way, to understand money, and make change. He was not wrong. But each time I won a pile of pennies and looked over at my twin brother's forlorn face, I gave him my pile of coins. Just like that, it didn't matter to me. Later, in a more consequential way, I dimmed my light often in an attempt to protect Joe from feeling weak or inferior. I loved and excelled at school, he did not. I was a star athlete in high school, he was not particularly interested in sports. I gave up on my mother early, he beat his head against her stony heart. Early on, he made significantly different choices than I did, which brought him under negative scrutiny from his teachers, parents and older brothers. We were joined at the hip as young children until we left for kindergarten at four years old. As December babies, we were launched early. He and I played outside, ate sandwiches on the front stoop, and took our baths together up until then. We had co-ed birthday parties and slept in the same bedroom in our early years. During kindergarten, we began to separate more; when I look at my Fort Couch kindergarten photo, I see a lonely and serious child. On December 3rd, 1991 I wrote this poem to myself.

My Kindergarten Child

You look back at me
from a kindergarten class photo
your shoulder length hair
sports a spit-curl above the right eye
wired down by a stretched out bobby-pin
and a haphazard ribbon.

Curly, wild hair standing out
a pyramid of sideways waves
more comical than you have ever been
funnier than what caused laughter to
bubble up in church or school
when the zealous priest
took himself to exalted places
and left you behind to laugh.

Tonight, on our birthday, I turn to you
even then, in kindergarten, at four
your thousand-year-old eyes
flash black as diamonds
shimmering and set in sadness.

I see you
and am so happy to say
you can call me Mother
I am ready for you at last.

I remember the very moment when I knew my twin and I were not one person. I loved kindergarten from the get-go. Our teacher smelled of roses and pressed powder. She was a big woman who squeezed me to her breasts in regular hugs. I sat on her abundant lap playing the piano during music time but, before that, we kids had to go into the closet-like room and pick an instrument for music hour. I always chose the triangle, but I regularly snuggled up on the teacher's lap on the piano stool ignoring the triangle. No doubt, she felt my hunger for affection and, as a good soul, gave it to me joyfully. Once when in that room picking out my triangle, I saw Joe kissing Suzanne Gleason. I was horrified and probably jealous. Horrified because Suzanne Gleason had a green, runny nose, and I couldn't imagine getting that close to her face. Jealous for the obvious reason that I thought Joe and I were a unit. That was the beginning of my separation from Joe, which only accelerated at the speed of light once it started. We were different in obvious ways and he was, of the two of us, my mother's clear favorite. He was a beautiful child and is a gorgeous man with emerald green eyes, fair skin, a strong cut jaw framed in black wavy hair. His notable intelligence has been compromised by trauma and tragedies. He does have a lyrical mind, which could have been brilliant, but it wanders in unruly ways. Sadly, he was mercilessly picked on by my two older brothers who, in any other household, may have been reprimanded by a vigilant mother and instructed otherwise. My mother turned a blind eye to it as did my father when he was home. My father modeled a concept of manhood in our household which included roughness and force; my mother was checked out and not present. Joe was not a happy child. I intervened more than once on his behalf as it was heartbreaking to watch, but I was ineffectual.

Too early on Joe had trauma at home. Though much of the story of his life remains unclear, there are disjointed narratives about his trips across the country. Sometimes there are temporal shifts when he's telling a story, which make those stories and his development hard to follow. Joe struggled further with two tragic accidents, one with a ferocious dog attack and later a crushing motorcycle accident both affecting the same leg. Understandably, he struggled with depression, bitterness and anger and then often asked too much of me; he wanted me to stay in Pittsburgh after his accident, which was more than I was willing to do. A mix of guilt and my will to survive accompanies my feelings toward Joe. Also, as finances are unequally distributed in my family, and my mother has given Joe money to live off of – tensions with both Joe and my mother grew.

With a mix of regret and happiness, I realize how lucky I am to have crawled out from under my mother's thumb in infancy. I don't know what the psychological term for it is, but I venture to maintain that if you remain tied and entwined with a sick parent you become sick yourself. Favoritism has its benefits, I'm sure, but I wouldn't know. I suspect it is more of a curse in most situations as the child is enmeshed in a cycle of psychological sickness and someone else in the family is getting hurt in the process. This is at least true in our family. In any event, my relationship to being a twin is riddled with loss and separation from birth to the time my mother sent Joe to military school in third grade, from his accidents to our innate differences.

So, back to 10th grade. This was a memorable year as I finally understood how to bypass the restrictions at home and step into my own shoes. I took my thoughts and feelings as seriously as Henry James had taken Isabel's in *The Portrait of a Lady*. I observed myself, my passions and precision in reading, living and gymnastics. My inner dialogue belied the consciousness of a capable, nervous and driven, unique and powerful young woman. I mounted the beam with a Russian split, pulled into a handstand, moved in a state of ecstatic absorption, and dismounted with an aerial back walkover, back flip to an applause that ripped through the silence and through the smallness of who I had once been. I was catapulted into living a conscious life full of intention, reverie and desire – mercifully yoked to discipline – just enough to realize my blueprint.

Catholic rhetoric and disdain best describes my mother's views on sex and intimacy, and though my father was often talking about and wanting sex, I learned nothing about the pleasures and risks of sexual intimacy. Even though I had "health class" and six older siblings, no information was transmitted. My siblings were mute on the subject or were just as clueless. Once I left home at 17 years old for Boston College, my sexual experiences with men began.

Unfortunately, the first time I had sex with a man, I got pregnant; I was not in love. I knew that telling my parents would be a waste of time as no solace or help would be forthcoming. In fact, I reckoned I would be coerced into carrying this child to term, which was not at all what I was willing to do. Two of my older siblings had suffered that fate, perhaps willingly but maybe out of a lack of real choice? I had a frightening, illegal abortion set up with the help of my friend Pam and her mother. I was met on a street corner by two six foot-plus black men and handed over my bundle of cash, $300 borrowed from Pam's mother. With that, I stepped into the car between them in the back seat and was immediately blindfolded. Driven to and led inside some basement somewhere, my blindfold was removed and the procedure took place on a dusty, dirty metal desk or table. The piercing, pinching, cramping pain was nearly unbearable. Without comfort and alone, I became numb with pain and fear. Blindfolded again, I was driven back to the same street corner and dropped off. It was a terrifying and dangerous illegal abortion. I walked back toward my dorm and, on the way, collapsed in tears on the hood of a hot, blue car in a grocery store parking lot. Inconsolable and alone, I struggled through the next five days in bed with a fever and missing classes. My anger welled up against the Catholic Church and my parents for the life threatening ignorance they handed me. I could have been murdered and raped and thrown off a bridge once I gave the cash. Instead, I was sick with a high fever and in pain; I could have died from the infection and/or permanently lost my fertility. I knew I was in big trouble. Pam got me in to see a gynecologist. With strong antibiotics and a proper D&C, I recovered with scar tissue in my fallopian tubes, which caused fertility complications. Wary about sex after that and painfully aware of how easy it is to make mistakes and how hard it was to fix them, I retreated from men. I was at a Catholic college as a result of a deal I had made with my mother. If allowed to go to a public high school rather than the Catholic alternative, I promised to attend a Catholic college. I was keen on honoring my word, so I went. Though it was not an ideal arrangement, it was a seminal experience which planted the seeds of feminism, pro choice, anti-organized religion, love and freedom that have grown steadily ever since. Also, the Jesuits know a thing or two about curriculum design and delivery; each of my classes were coordinated in that the history of art, music, language and philosophy/religion went through time together. I received an amazing foundational education that first year.

It wasn't until I left Boston College and transferred to the University of Wisconsin, Madison to complete my undergraduate degree that I began to reach out to men again. This was a successful chapter of first boyfriends, tenderness and sexual experience. Once again, I thank my father as he played a significant role in my core belief that sexuality was pleasurable, good for you, and necessary. I share his opinions and, as a child of the 60s, I live my life seeking and expressing my sexual energy freely.

Catholicism and its dogmatic authority structure didn't

work for me, try as I might. I remember taking my "holy communion" and lingering at the altar rail waiting to feel the supposed holiness of taking in the body of Christ, but where was the feeling? It was a lie, I concluded, as I did not receive a mystical experience like the many I had already known even at seven years old. There was no magic, no rush, no energetic shift up there at the altar to justify the hype and the accompanying angelic-white dress and veil. My mother, no doubt embarrassed, retrieved me and walked me away from the altar. No one bothered to ask why I lingered so long at the altar but, in truth, I would not have been capable of verbalizing my young reasoning, as it lived in those undisclosed inner-chambers of thought. In retrospect, I know I recognized the holy and the sacred but not in a traditional way, not at the altar in a Catholic Church.

When John Gardner in his remarkable novel *Grendel* explains how one of the most terrifying monsters in the English language describes his consciousness and process of knowing, I can relate: *Half awake, half asleep, I felt as if I were myself the cave, my thoughts coursing downward through my own strange hollows …or some impulse older and darker than thought, as old as the mindless mechanics of a bear, the twilight meditations of a wolf, a tree....*

There is no flattery in comparing myself to a brutal beast, yet I cannot deny that Gardner's description hit a nerve that rings true. I have no difficulty admitting to and enjoying my animal nature though in me it exists without cruelty; no doubt, something archetypal and primeval is at work when perception merges with sensation. This came strongly into play when birthing, breast feeding and loving my daughters, for example, which again made my mother's damaging lack of instinct and interest in me unbearable. It came so easily to me, and I remain grateful that I got my father's hotline into animal energies.

Sex and physicality in general continue to play a prominent role in my understanding of how personal, energetic flow affected everything about me: perception, creativity, energy, identity, romantic love, and friendship. Other examples I remember include learning to ride my red Schwinn bicycle around the block without ever touching the handlebars – at least a mile in distance with four corners. It took all summer to master this task. The bike and I were one; its tilt was my tilt. Other times, venturing to Pop Shram's, a local recreation spot, was a destination where I would jump on the trampoline and practice archery. I also enjoyed doing cartwheels on the lawn and walking the fields and valleys, creeks and forests of our neighborhood: doses of energy medicine. I sought solitude and ecstasy; I was not taught to fear strangers or the wild creatures of the woods. Fortunately, nothing untoward happened as I wandered alone for hours. I do remember a stare-down with a red fox – fear and communion – and the whisper of branches as it disappeared back into the woods.

What a pleasure to have wandered alone to destinations of my choice, indeed a luxury to have grown up at a time when the world was a safer place to let a child explore on their own. Neglect and profound loneliness also figure into the picture, but nonetheless few children have this opportunity in today's world. Since I survived unharmed, I look back on explorations without an adult interpreting my experiences as a rare and imprinting gift.

After the mastery of Mumbly Peg and *gamedances*, more complex challenges came along, and I bit them off one by one. In high school, I achieved high status as a gymnast; it demanded precision, physicality, aesthetic control of my body and a defined sense of beauty in how the body arcs and flows. On top of my academic and athletic practice load, I still insisted on learning how to sew in Home Economics. I was on "the college track" thanks to my teachers, guidance counselor and my PSAT scores. I practiced gymnastics for four hours everyday after school into the evening and had to bum rides home; no one wanted to pick me up. But for reasons I cannot explain, I insisted on Home Ec, as it was called, and sewing held a thrill for years. It demanded exactness and aesthetic vision. There is a level of mimicry in sewing, in the use of patterns and then the free-fall of choosing the fabric, stiff and crisp linen or diaphanous, gauzy silks. Years later, I picked cream colored silk and lace and sewed my wedding dress from an Emanuel Ungaro pattern, a Hungarian dress designer. On that project, I only let myself sew for a few hours each day and in the morning before work, as the patience and precision demands were well known to me. High standards excited me and drove me to set my sights higher and higher. When pregnant, I used the remnants from my wedding dress to sew a take-home dress for my first daughter, Amanda. It was way too big, but mine and hers, which was what mattered. When Deva was born, she too wore this dress, and it was mine and hers too.

I created and serviced high standards, but I didn't know why or how? No one in my household was a fashionista to be sure, and no one sewed or knitted or did any other handcraft. Though my older sisters were majorettes and cheerleaders, this was not an individual sport. My mother did nothing well. When she made a bed, it was lumpy and lacked the crisp luster of a well-made bed. Laundry was not folded carefully, and the pots and pans she washed still had a filmy-greasy feel to them. My father did most of the grocery shopping, much of the cooking and earned a living. My mother did not get her driver's license until 1952 when I was three years old. Dad did not do any housework. He did have a refined sense of beauty: the Carrara marble tiles with red grout and the field stone exterior of our home are some prominent examples. The other unexpected role he played is that he could have invented the current "Color Me Beautiful" approach to dressing. Daddy would take us down to the fabric district and line us up with bolts of fabric at his fingertips. He would go daughter by daughter and holding bolts of color against our skin would declare what color we should and should not wear. No yellow for me and never Kelly green. Red, black and white were my colors and still are! He also cautioned that our skin tone would change once we got our periods, and we would have to revisit the color wheel. My father dressed my mother in the early years of their marriage; the dashing hats and hemlines seen in these early photographs are to his credit. He wanted a "babe" and because my mother was tall and good looking, he dolled her up. Maybe Dad was a fashionista! Later the wrapping paper quality of her wardrobe diminished along with the spell he held over her.

Learning to sew was amazing! I begged for a sewing machine so I could work at home and not just at school. Eventually, I made clothes for myself and my sisters just to get practice in adding sleeves and zippers. I had talent – the teacher remarked – I wanted my own sewing machine, but after multiple refusals from my mother, I had to take matters into my own hands. I was fifteen and too young to hold a job, but I went up to the F.W. Woolworth Company's five-and-dime store and applied for a job, lying about my age. I pulled it off and got the job – no ride to work, of course, but I found a way. I can still remember the many times I went through Woolworth's front doors, passed the food counter up front, and noted the ragtag bunch of diners on red vinyl stools eating lunch or supper alone. Maybe I could relate to their loneliness and felt at home when I came through the front doors of the Woolworth's five and dime? I was there alone, in defiance of my obstacle-creating mother, in order to get what I wanted and needed. With my first several pay checks, working on the weekends, I earned the $67.50 I needed to get a used Singer sewing machine at the thrift store. Meanwhile, on our Christmas trips to Hornes Department Store, one older sister would milk my parents for cashmere sweaters and an alligator purse and shoes. I resented her materialism and her insolence.

Other sisters were modest in their choice of presents. After all, "we're not the Mellons or the Rockefellers," my dad reminded us often. There were eight of us and one bread winner. My father had the Midas Touch, as does my brother, Ed, but still…I was sensitive to the financial demands placed on my father. One child's greed deprived the rest of us of anything and, if my father tightened up visibly as my sister insisted, I winced too. Early on, I saw my mother in certain siblings and my father in others. I picked up on the downcast eyes and all of the copious verbal and nonverbal communications. I know now just how hard I worked to keep it all in check: engage my empathy while protecting myself from insensitivity, negativity and over-simplifications. This is another skill that serves me well in my current profession and another instance that brings up how my life schooled me in necessary ways. I kept that job throughout high school and, ever interested in exotic fashion, bought a weird Lynx-like jacket at the thrift store and my black and white, Grecian prom dress at Saks Fifth Avenue. I might add that I wore my hair in a sweep-over style that I thought looked snazzy; it didn't! Or, it sure doesn't look great now when I see it in old photos.

In my senior year, we went prom shopping, and I wanted that Cleopatra-like dress. Mother said no but offered a certain amount of money for prom dresses, pretending there really was an established budget for such a thing. I quickly regrouped because I wanted THAT dress, but didn't want to be thoughtless or greedy. So, I kept my job and worked extra hours to make up the difference. I wore that dress to the prom with a guy I barely remember named Owen, but I remember the dress well.

Currently, as an adult, there is a side of me that wants to participate in loose exploration and another side that craves mastery and the safety it provides. Exploration requires freedom, and mastery requires both discipline and structure. Though I don't experience these pulling urges as opposites but rather the push and pull of body and spirit, I often struggle to find the right life circumstances to allow for both. These urges and cravings cannot be put on a clock or in a planner; they show up on a frequently rotating basis and call me to attention. Perhaps more of a paradox than conflictual, this tension is as much a part of me as my curly hair and shows up in work and love, both essential parts of my journey. Luckily, I have been able to design my own career to support my need for both freedom and discipline. In my desire for the right romantic partner, I often feel strain and exasperation as I cannot *design* a man the way I've designed my work life. On the one hand, I love a yummy man capable of deep intimacy and, on the other, I can only respect a man who is called toward his interior, to solitude, creativity, and absorption in something beyond me and the mundane responsibilities of life. Still, in my limited and disappointing experiences, when a need for freedom exists in the men I have known, it often wanders into flagrant womanizing and other self-absorbed behaviors. I have suffered betrayals both in and out of marriage; the pain is deep and defining, and I continue to explore my contributions to relationship dynamics including my attachment issues. Not experiencing maternal unconditional love as a child, my deficits can be burdensome to my lovers. It is now easy for me to see how my strands of interests and personality traits hang together: physical, psychological, metaphysical, and sexual expression originating in and enhancing eros brought me a sense of connection to something beyond myself. A capacity for absorption brought me into experiences head-on and kept me there long enough to learn and gain mastery. I now recognize the pattern or recipe that brings on these explosive experiences: let nature seduce me into reverie until I get dreamy, at which point the active and mesmerizing side of eros rises up in me.

Returning to my mother and how her relationship to herself, her family, her husband, her other children and me played itself out in my life, there is still much to be told. We do not have an easy or good relationship. She is the most damaged person in my upbringing, and yet she presides over one of the most primal of relationships. The uncertainties and path of denial in my mother's life cause many of her complications and my complications with her. My mother is still alive and "well" at 100 years old. She lives alone in a brick house in Jacksonville, Florida, near her favorite child, Sam. Our family consists of five girls and three boys: Peggy, Jane, Carole, Sam, Ed, Pat, me and Joe. Sam is the oldest son and my father's namesake.

My mother's story deserves to be told as it is intriguing and odd; I will tell the version I know, which I heard from my father and mother by word of mouth and may not be the true story. The McGann family's reputed wealth came from the paving and bootlegging businesses – the latter, an area of competition with my father. They had a live-in maid, Molly, and horse stables. One version of her history says that her mother, Elizabeth, married a Russian or German or French and maybe Jewish horse groomer or street paver, who worked for the McGann family. This worker was not considered a good match for a woman who had promise and breeding, especially not by my Grandma Lizzie's mother, Mary McGann. In spite of and maybe because of the resistance, Elizabeth pursued this star-crossed love and married Charles Guyion, who was rumored and later admitted to being a drinker and a gambler. From the McGann point of view, he was unsuitably "other" by nationality and class. How much of this is true or prejudiced, racist rumor is unclear, but my mother's attitude toward her father does not revoke this hearsay.

When my mother was born to this couple, her mother, Elizabeth, hoped to move into the family home on Reed Street, on "the hill" in Soho, but Pete McGann, Elizabeth's brother, had beaten and said he'd kill Charles if he came near. First my mother was given to her Aunt Mary McGann then, at school age, she moved in with her grandmother, another Mary McGann. Elizabeth continued to live near her husband, Charles, and with her first born daughter, Mazie. Her grandmother, Mary McGann, was now a widow and lived with her son, John, in the Reed Street house. My mother was unknowingly raised by surrogate parents: her grandmother and her Uncle John. She claims to have been visited daily by her mother, whom she thought was her aunt. Lizzie (Elizabeth) would visit her daughter on her way back from work as a nutritionist in the local hospital. At one point, Charles reputedly moved to Virginia then back again to Pittsburgh during which time my mother was conceived. Mazie, mother's sister, was about four years older. Mother thought Mazie was her cousin until she was 16. The Shakespearean plays that explore identity swapping resemble this mess. My mother had no fondness for Mazie maybe because she was jealous of the attention and care she received naturally from Elizabeth and then perhaps heightened due to the polio Mazie had contracted as a child. Right up until Mazie's death, my mother criticized her, her marriage and her son, Howie. The echo of Mazie's polio affected all of us as my mother would not let us spend time in swimming pools nor did any of us learn to swim as children because she believed you could get polio in swimming pools. Grandma Lizzie died at 51 years old of a cerebral hemorrhage brought on by untreated high blood pressure; she was buried on the day my mother gave birth to her first son, Sam. Perhaps my mother's favoritism was influenced by this exchange of places between Sam and Lizzie: birth and burial inevitably bring heightened energy and emotion.

Mother grew up having been told her father had first abandoned Lizzie, and later died when mother was two years old. When she was in her early 50s, married with eight children, she received a phone call from her father, Charles. He was dying and the hospital called my mother as they knew she had married Sam Easton and looked her up through the Easton name. Margaret was furious: "You are no father of mine. Where were you when I needed you?" She refused to acknowledge Charles Guyion as her father or to visit him. Still, she was dragged by a few of my siblings to meet him in Mayview, a state hospital where he was both living and dying. He had been picked up as a homeless vagrant and had become a ward of the state. Another version of the story my father repeatedly told was that Charles was alive and living in Mayview; this flew in the face of his notion of family. He hinted that the McGann clan, out of hatred for Charles, had used their influence to have him committed for life to this state hospital and that was unfathomable to my father. Upon Charles' death, mother was asked by the hospital if she wanted to bury her father and she said, "no, give his body to science so at least he'll have done some good on this earth." If this is in fact true, we need look no further for the source of my mother's sinister nature.

Like much of her history, my mother's maiden name and ethnicity are still up for grabs. Most of her eight children have questions about her maiden name and, therefore, our ancestry on her side. Margaret Veronica McGann as a name and legacy are under scrutiny all the time. Here's a quick study of the confusions: Margaret Guyion is how my mother's birth certificate reads. She took her middle name, Veronica, of her own choosing. It was her confirmation name and also the name of a friend who died young. The maiden surname she used – McGann – came from her maternal grandmother's lineage. As her grandmother, Mary McGann raised her, this makes some inherent sense. McGann also rings of the Irish, so that suited her family. The only other paternal relative who figures into this is Lina, my paternal great-grandmother on my mother's side. As the story goes, she was my mother's father's French or Russian or German or Jewish mother, who visited my own mother when she was a child. My mother claims that she spoke French and lived and worked as a nurse in London, so French? As mother was told her father was dead and, when he surfaced, she refused to believe he was her father, so I suppose it's not a surprise that she didn't carry his name. Or, just as likely, her maternal grandmother just enrolled her in school and called her Margaret McGann. Confused? We eight children certainly were and still are, as all aspects of my mother's paternal ancestry are muddled, though she denies the squabble by denying her father his parentage: Margaret McGann it is!

My mother possesses many characteristics that stir grave misgivings in me. First, her Catholic faith runs deep, and she escapes reality regularly by leaping into prayer instead of thought. Her "give it to God" looks to me like an excuse not to feel or think. Though I value and respect each person's embrace of the tenets of their faith, as a child and an adult, my mother's lack of engagement around a question or an idea leaves a gaping hole. Together with the other aspects of her character, this raises suspicion in me.

Her denial is legendary and like many untreated, traumatized children, she hasn't faced the abandonment issues in her childhood, much less with the tenderness and care that would be required to work through such profound scars and then proceed to pass tenderness forward onto her children. Hers is a story of unsanctioned love, cut off, disavowals, denial, lies, secrets, prejudices and hurts packaged by my mother like a gift in shiny wrapping paper that says 'everything in my life was perfect.' When my mother was 83 years old, she had a dream in which she was rattling around in her childhood home looking for her mother's bedroom. She couldn't find it and awoke, realizing for the first time that she had never lived with her mother. "My childhood was beautiful," she always says, "I went to school in handmade pinafores and braided hair and had piano lessons."

Unschooled in love, she became a negative and critical adult, believing her "honesty" to be illuminating when it was decidedly dart-sharp and hurtful. Often she uses platitudes, which came across as banal and thoughtless like, "a good loser is a loser." This saying was used when our many competitions broke down into winners and losers. The bad losers got attention from this saying and the winners got nothing. The kids on a losing streak in life got the greatest share of my mother's attention, love, and, eventually, money. As I was already having original ideas and truly thought I had something to say, I very soon stopped listening to what my mother said as it felt flat and hollow to me. Limited, limiting, and critical to a fault, my mother had and has no friends. She lavished her criticisms on our neighbors one-by-one as with my father's family. My sister, Pat, reacted to this aspect of my mother's character, much as I did to mother's insipidness and sloppiness; Pat vowed to have many friends as an adult woman, and I practiced perfectionism in areas of thought, creativity and orderliness.

We need no psychology text book to recognize that the bonding between mother and child was neither initiated nor sustained in my case. I have no memory of being held or cherished by my mother. She was intolerant of any show of emotion: tears, laughter, passion, exuberance, and she was exhausted most of the time with little patience for questions. Becoming a mother of eight children in 16 years has got to wear you out. When we came home from school, she was often on the couch with her feet up watching a favorite TV show. Decidedly, I fit the description of her perfect nightmare child: I could and did *get going* over many of my passions from reading to gymnastics, from sewing to wandering and journaling, from endless questions to fervent religious doubt. She was and remains a major naysayer and suppressor in my life. In the many astrological charts I have had drawn on my behalf over the years, the Pluto moon aspects in my natal chart indicate that I showed up as a catalyst for my mother's unconscious fears and frustrations with the potential to create a devastating mother/daughter dynamic where I might rightly view my mother as a threat and associate danger and abandonment with love. In any event, my mother tried to wield power and control over me and offered me no comfort, so the life long task of learning to honor my own emotional needs has been a challenge.

Whether in the stars or not, my mother has a truck load of issues and biases that rained down on all of us. My earliest encounter of real consequence with her iron fist was when I was recruited by the prestigious SOKAL, a Russian gymnastics organization. Right around the start of 10th grade, I had made it to Nationals as a gymnast for Upper St. Clair High School leading to the recruitment. I was burning with pride and desire, but my mother flatly refused to even consider it. I can still hear her saying, "You have too many muscles already. It's not ladylike. Look at your legs! This Russian place is on the other side of Pittsburgh, and I'm not going to shuttle you across town and wait there while you jump around." Not only was I furious at being thwarted, but she had to hurl an insult into the mix? I thought my legs were looking good. So much for a mother reflecting one's beauty. I didn't yet learn that showing *joie de vivre* was equivalent to the kiss of death as my mother reigns as the Queen of Repression. Ever the kill joy, she silenced my voice and stifled my agency, or at least she tried. I see this then and now as the very abuse and neglect that fired my will and discipline to step into selfhood, leave home young, and live beyond her. In retrospect, the lessons and the harvest are quite simply my essence, much of it good, but it is not always easy being me.

Despite my clear-eyed opinion of her, my mother wanted power and control over us and my father; in their relationship, the seesaw hung in her favor and in her direction. She considered herself and her family superior to his and never let that narrative die. As a product of a poor, immigrant family, my father hustled for his livelihood and may have internalized her racism and the racism in this country. As such, he had no rebuttal when Margaret looked down her nose at him. On those Sunday evenings when our Lebanese family visited, my mother was invisible. She justified her behavior by reminding us, again, of her refinement. It's also true, though, that she had no love for my father's family. She had had to live with Nagibi, her mother-in-law to be, for six months before their marriage to learn how to cook and be a "good wife." She resented Nagibi, my grandmother, for this stint, and his family for their loud and passionate ways. In this way, my mother has some feminist fervor, and she resented the role she was forced into by a tradition not her own. To her credit, the five of us girls may not have gone to college and may still be licking envelopes in a shop and married to some rich and oppressive man had it not been for her insistence. On the flip side, as a mostly defiant person, if Dad said black, she said white. If he wanted us traditional and married, then she did what she could to defy his authority; it wasn't all about us, but her defiance of him also played a role.

I felt her racism then and know it to be true now. My mother's favorite children are those who resemble her most – blue or green-eyed and fair-skinned. Add narcissism to piety and racism and you have a whopping cocktail of repression and control justified by morality. She believed her own narrative and reinforced her sense of superiority by favoring the ones who resembled her most. I was not one of those and experienced my mother as a deadly enemy to my life force. My father's Lebanese gusto often collided with my Irish mother's tightness and coldness: the bi-ethnic tension at play. We grew up in the wake of this tension, which often boiled into raging physical fighting in their bedroom at night. It is interesting to me that my feminism and experience as a grown woman and a mother has not created more sympathy for my mother. In fact, I am less able to tolerate or imagine the kind of favoritism and cruelty that my mother still subscribes to in her interactions with her children and her opinion of almost everyone she encounters: neighbors, caregivers, and in-laws. Her cold heartedness is unfathomable to me. I align myself once again with Isabel Archer: *...that the chance of inflicting a sensible injury upon another person, presented only as a contingency, caused her at moments to hold her breath. That always seemed to her the worst thing that could happen to one. On the whole, reflectively, she was in no uncertainty about the things that were wrong. She had no taste for thinking of them, but whenever she looked at them fixedly she recognized them. It was wrong to be mean, to be jealous, to be false, to be cruel...*

My father, Sam, was 28 and Margaret was 16 years old when they married. He was an experienced man of the world, and she was a sheltered, Catholic young girl. He was mesmerized by her beauty: "Black Irish." Certain photographs of my mother reveal strength and contrast. She had, when he met her, see-through, icy-blue eyes, jet-black hair, and alabaster-white skin. Later, he lurked outside of school and drove Margaret home in his fancy car. By then he was bootlegging and rich. The facts of their union, however, are clouded. My mother still hides her marriage certificate saying "I told you he stole me." She wonders aloud about whether she was perhaps given to Dad by her Aunt Myra in some evening-of-the-score bootlegging deal. He did ask and receive her mother, Elizabeth's consent, who found him charming and agreed to the marriage. He knew the family as he visited their neighborhood in earlier days with his cart and horse, Bob. My mother admits to liking the shape of his head but nothing more. Most probably, my father lied about her age saying she was 21. It would have been illegal at the time to marry a 16 year old. There's a creepiness to this story not lost on me; he hustled her. But still, between the two of them, he was far easier to love.

Though there was chemistry between my parents in their early years, mother described sex and orgasm in the rare moments she discussed this kind of thing as disgusting as a "cold and a sneeze"(respectively). In distorting a religious concept of the body as a mere shell-like home for the spirit, she once said to me that "the body is garbage." With my love of movement and physicality, how could we see eye-to-eye? Perhaps as another response to childhood trauma, she lived disconnected from her body as a source of pleasure and comfort. For me, the body became my refuge perhaps an alternative response to trauma. I expressed myself and reveled in the artful use of my body: moving to music, exploding into cartwheels on the beach, leaning into corners on my bike, aerial back walkovers on the balance beam, all of which were a source of joy, self-expression, and solace for me.

Her love/hate and often degrading view of my father lasted for most of their 63 year marriage with a few years of separation when she moved to Orlando, Florida after I left for college. Her scornful disregard, as mentioned, was also projected onto the Easton family of origin and the children who resembled them most: I am one of those! My father, on the other hand, built his life around the love for his family. He worked to support his mother and to provide well for his wife and his eight children. He showed no favoritism, and though deceased now, we all know he would be mighty angry to learn how my mother has continued, unchecked by him, to create such strife among us. My beloved brother, Ed, is our living patriarch and carries on my father's sense of family, which is a mitigating factor working against the divisiveness of my mother's favoritism. Of late, however, the annual family reunions he hosts are not attended by my mother nor my brother Sam due to ongoing rifts.

Mother has psychic qualities that come through dreams. Famously, she heard her mother in a dream say "watch that boy's eye." And the next day, my mother prevented a fall where Sam would have seriously hurt his left eye. When pregnant with us, mother dreamed she would have twins and name them Wayne and Blaine. She made these our middle names as they had no hint of saintliness, which she required in a first name. Whatever the source, psychic premonition or superstition, I once saw a connection between my capacities and hers. I dream vividly, but I am not predominantly a dreamer and my transcendent moments do not hold premonitory content. So, with time and age, I slowly came to feel that my psychic gifts were of a different ilk than hers.

She is a nervous, chatty person, who does more talking out loud than communicating. She is righteous and brassy-minded out of defiance rather than authentic convictions. She loves church and bingo, which are her social life. The frequent exercise of favoritism and power set up adversarial relationships among us as children. Though not a stupid woman, she is uneducated and narcissistic. She didn't like her studies at Sacred Heart High School and quit after two years to attend cosmetology school. It is unclear whether or not she finished her schooling; she was married at 16 and pregnant soon after.

By far, mother is not the physical, nurturing love-bug-of-a-mother that I would have wished for and needed and, as such, I rejected her early on and she knew it. I have a nose for disingenuous people, and I believe her to be one. Furthermore, she was nasty and withholding to my father, whom I loved, understood and believed to be a good man. He had his faults, but he appeared to me to be twisted around the hub of her torturing negativity and power trips. She was and still is particularly unkind to me as well and kept me down and back and under as best she could. In her words, I was "too much," "asked too many questions," and was "an oversexed pepper-pot." Mother added invisibility to being "too much" and, with that, I was effectively silenced as a child. In very significant ways, I took heart and soul underground, so to speak, and most of what I loved became clandestine. My thoughts, dreams, longings and, virtually my lifeblood, were held and safe inside of diaries and cigar boxes. I kept a journal and hid it; I had a large cigar box under my bed full of treasures I found outdoors in my wanderings: a robin's egg so tenderly jagged and famously blue; a few smooth stones from the river I crossed on my way to Pop Shram's; a pair of pinecones joined on one stem. My father loved his aromatic Cuban cigars and there was no shortage of those decorative cedar boxes with "gold" fasteners. I still have a stack on my bedside table and continue my love and affection for them. As I got older, my mother's tactics changed to overt control and cruel criticism. Just last year she said over the phone to me, "Peggy's pointing to me to tell me to tell you that I love you – you know I do, right?" Her lack of genuine feeling for me came through so sharply, it took my breath away. I left the rhetorical question hanging as these kind of shocking utterances deserve nothing more than stunned silence.

The insecurity under the narcissist's skin is what I have come to call a double disability. I would feel sorry for her if I could; I would forgive her if she ever attempted some self-knowledge or improved slightly, but she is deep-down unlovable in my book. I often wonder what has transpired in her during her 100 year tenure on planet Earth since she appears to have learned very little.

Add to the distaste, my mother smelled of urine and Clorox throughout my childhood, her hands of Clorox from washing up the sink and her pants reeked of pee. Her *uber-white* body, the few times I caught a glimpse, sagged and buckled un-attractively even in her 30s. I was repulsed, and I still recoil with an involuntary hesitation when I see her, wondering if I might gag involuntarily when she gets too close. I often think if she had at least been a bit of a drinker, some of the best in the Irish might have leaked out...no such luck! Gardner again: *She hurls herself across the void and buries me in her bristly fur and fat. I sicken with fear...Her flesh is loose. Buried under my mother I cannot see. She smells of wild pig and fish.* In this and the earlier Gardner quote, Grendel stirred in me a realization of how one generation evolves beyond the first and so on. His mother had no language and Grendel could understand and use language; this brought him a bit further from beast and closer to human. Being one evolutionary step beyond his mother caused a chasm between him and his mother and much suffering. There is something in his revulsion and his confusion about what he understood compared to his mother, along with her physical characteristics that resonates with me.

I realized early that I had progressed past the point where my mother ended. Happily, this is not true in regards to my father, which intensifies my connection to him then and now. As to my mother, however, and almost from crib time forward, I knew I could not eat at her table, and pushed away forcibly. Unlike my twin brother and my immediately older sister, I did not clamor or beg for my mother's love and respect. Early on, I knew and, more remarkably, accepted that in every possible meaningful way, Margaret was not my mother. My will to thrive informed this response; it was a necessity. Nonetheless, I have suffered as any child would who did not have a loving and protective mother, someone to see my beauty, teach me things and usher me into autonomy. Indeed, I feel like a victorious survivor, a fact which informs my identity and voice.

No doubt my mother's convoluted and virtually parentless history may be at the heart of her guarded and stingy capacity to love, but the damage she in turn wrought, was equally striking. She is almost a cardboard figure as her malignant predictability informed her actions and her decisions lifelong. The final gesture of her loveless disposition was to draft her Final Will and Testament and circulate it to each of the eight of us in 2006. Her favorite son, Sam, is to receive all assets, absolute power of attorney over her life, finances, and end-of-life care. Despite collective horror and unified voices of pleading and reasoning from the essentially orphaned seven other living children, she and Sam, a childless Vietnam Vet, chose to preserve and protect the will as it stands. Pleading letters and emails flew back and forth to no avail. In having redrafted my will recently, the comparison was in profound contrast. I wrote the following: *My daughters, I love you both unconditionally and eternally. Tending to your welfare has been an honor and a blessing. Please take what I have left to give in support of lives filled with conscious intention, active compassion with the blessings and grace to fulfill those intentions. Above all else, set your compass and your watch by one another. May what I give be in support of your individual expressions of life, for your love for one another, the Earth and all your loved ones.*

Since this expresses my credo, it is easy to see why I struggle to understand an apparent lack of motherly jubilance and fairness. My struggle is not about money or greed; it is simply about longing to have a protective and equal love from one's mother. For me, her decision operates entirely on a psychological and emotional plane. Mother's decision to divide her estate unequally with preferential treatment to one child is her credo. Hard as it is! Note, she did not choose to posthumously reveal her will, so it is fair to look at it as a provocation. It is not uncharacteristic of her to drop a bomb and then leave the room pretending to wonder what could have possibly caused such a stir. After a life with a cold and self-absorbed mother, I do not hope for a change of heart and mind – no metanoia on my part. Like Faulkner's Quentin from *The Sound and the Fury* concludes: *If I'd just had a mother so I could say Mother Mother."* So too, I come to this same conclusion. I intend her will to stand as my mother's final opportunity to abuse and neglect me.

Eight children were born in 16 years to a Lebanese father and a mother mostly Irish and mixed descent. The early years of their marriage appear to have had been happy with good sexual energy and a positive, family building quality, the two oldest siblings, Margaret Mary (Peggy) and Jane testify. The next three, Carole, Sam and Ed, were caught up more than once in the nexus of our parents chronic fighting, which always began at night in the bedroom – no wonder! The final three, Pat, myself and Joe, rarely slept through the night as the fighting and tension grew worse with time causing slammed and locked doors and loud screams. I was not so much afraid for myself as I was confused and disappointed by my parents, who turned into monstrous creatures in the night (like Grendel). My older brothers and sisters ran interference sometimes, and I felt that layer of protection plus my father had never turned his rage on me. I do remember coming home from grade school and wondering if I would find my mother dead. I am also marked by an early memory of being brought into their room one middle-of-the-night and held around the shoulders by my sister, Peggy, my tiny feet bent over the footboard and my eyes bouncing between my yelling half-naked parents and the serene painting of Chinese figures fishing on the headboard of their bed. I guess the frequency of these fights made such a traumatic encounter inevitable.

Along with some of the other exotic furnishings in our home, my parents had a hand-painted bedroom set from China. The set included two dressers, a bed, and a dressing table with mirror. Each piece was painted a golden yellow color with various hand-painted scenes from China: pointed mountains, fishing canoes on a river, and men and women plowing fields behind yoked steers. In another scene, a couple had a wooden yoke on their shoulders, balancing and carrying water in two buckets. These paintings had a foreign and bucolic feel especially when contrasted with the ugly fighting in the bedroom that night. The bed had a slightly curled headboard and footboard and the dressing table had a triptych mirror. In response to a scene I could not digest, I tried to escape into the Chinese landscape instead of watching my parents but, when looking away, I could see my forlorn reflection in triptych. This is a scrambled, disjointed and indelible memory. No doubt, I didn't have an ideal childhood, and I have a host of issues to prove it, some of which have risen and been quieted by therapy, age, love, motherhood, and spiritual practice. As Bessel Van Der Kolk, M.D. says, ... *it helps to have grown up with steady and predictable parents; parents who delight in you, in your discoveries and explorations; parents who helped you organize your comings and goings; and who served as role models for self-care and getting along with other people.*

My parents were caught up in their own drama when not providing and cooking for a brood of offspring; often I felt like an afterthought, especially because I was good and independent: the seventh child. What pain I still carry doesn't ache the way it once did, though I do occasionally give into bouts of disbelief, self pity and wondering. The self pity and wondering I sometimes experience comes from questioning who I might be today had I had a modicum of support and conscious love. My father's love was essential to my well being, but I also know it was more tribal than individualized. From a reincarnation/karmic perspective, I chose this setup, including my parents in order to do necessary soul work, which I continue to attempt to do – I like the agency in this view of life.

I remember asking and answering my own questions as there was no one there to provide information, so inevitable distortions arose. When trying to understand how the radio worked, for example, I observed that at Mary Lou Walsh's house across the street, I heard Beethoven and at my house I heard Porgy Chedwick playing the current hits like *The Twist* and *Smoke Gets in Your Eyes*. I concluded that the radio in each house played something else, and I tried to prove my theory by going into the Hodder house and the DeVilling mansion to test it out. Yep, each house had a different tune. Only years later did I understand the notion of radio stations.

When I was around six years old, my pet turtle died. My twin or my mother had flushed Josie down the toilet, which I learned when I went to the shallow plastic bowl to get Josie out to play. She was gone. The turtle water was gone and what was left was a dingy water-ring and a green plastic palm tree. I ran back and forth between the toilet and her bowl in disbelief as Joe let me know that Josie had been flushed down the toilet. Joe said, "Her arms and legs were all pulled in – "she was dead." "That's how Josie sleeps," I corrected him with my hand cupped in memory of holding her stone-like body. I sobbed and still remember how cold the tile felt under my bare feet. Each morning for months, I sprinkled a bit of flaky turtle food down the toilet for Josie. I had no idea how death or sewage systems worked and imagined her swimming around down there with a pack of other creatures and finding the food I sent her daily. I remember he and my mother snickering about me because I couldn't grasp the concept of death.

There was so much I didn't understand and sometimes this led to ridicule by authorities or outright danger like when I shoved two round steel ball bearings up my nose. These round metal balls were the same size as my perfectly round nostrils: a good fit. My brothers called me "NoseAnne." Again, left alone with all kinds of potentially hazardous materials, I was experimenting. In short order, I realized I couldn't get them out of my nose. I jumped around hoping they'd come out to no avail. Eventually, I ran upstairs to the kitchen to tell my mother as I was beginning to feel afraid. She complained about how inconvenient it was to get me to the eye-ear-nose-and-throat doctor, Dr. McCarthy, who's office was far away. Again, no comfort, no soothing words but rather the message that I was inconveniencing her, which I was, I'm sure. She had other kids to take care of and dinner to cook. This message of inconvenience coupled with her refrain, "You are too much," describes how my mother felt about me. I got the "too much" retort when I asked my questions like, "Why is a spoon called a spoon and a fork called a fork," who decided that?" She didn't have the patience nor the intellect to deal with my steady inquiries.

I remember being alone in the back seat while mother drove me to Dr. McCarthy's. We were in the waiting room when the doctor came out to get us and simultaneously, a big dog entered the waiting room. It was a large German Shepherd with a mask and, in fright, I jumped up on the waiting room couch. In that moment, the ball bearings streamed out of my nose and bounced onto the wooden floor. I was so happy not to have a procedure done to me, but my mother was not so happy and reprimanded me for making her drive all that way for nothing.

Continuing with my confusion and ignorance, I also thought that getting a new car was a yearly event for everybody. My father had a fixation with cars and did his wheeling and dealing to bring home a shiny black Buick convertible with red leather interior for his wife and a cobalt blue Chevy 409 for my brother, Sam, for his 16th birthday. I learned to drive on that Chevy and navigated the yellowed tile tunnels called the "Liberty Tubes" in my father's weirdly pink Cadillac. I clearly remember how my skinny, muscled leg quivered trying to man-age that nine-spring clutch and the lurching 409 powerhouse and, later, wrecking the Cadillac when driving with my brother's friend, Barry Queer. I don't remember how that came about, but I hid behind my locked door and negotiated peace with my father before throwing the latch and opening the door. I was terrified. Where was my mother in this moment and so many other moments? Why didn't she come to my rescue? I was such a good kid, always, that having inadvertently crossed the line didn't feel too safe. As always though, my father listened kindly, knew Barry had put me up to the adventure, and realized that a big-finned Cadillac was way too big for a physically small, beginner driver to handle. Maybe Barry and Ed took a hit for me, who knows? These dazzling cars made me think we were rich, another distortion at least in relative terms. My father's car craze came from his past: the stellar mobster rides he either saw, rode in or owned in his past as a bootlegger. He could describe the fenders and headlights of the Rolls Royce *Silver Ghost*, the luxury Pierce-Arrow sedan driven by stars and tycoons alike, and, of course the Lincoln Continental and Cadillac. He never let go of that love; in fact, when he aged out of driving, he was crushed.

Loneliness is part of my life, which may be the single most important resume item for a writer/artist, or so I tell myself. My heightened sensibilities set me apart in remarkable and challenging ways and something always pointed me inward toward reflection. My childhood provided enough emotional turmoil for a dozen novels. The irony of feeling lonely in a bustling household and being a twin 'taboot' is not lost on me. Sometimes I struggled to understand how this could be possible: more questions. When I read Jack Kornfield's *A Path With Heart*, I made significant headway in understanding this phenomena. *I have always had difficulty with loneliness. I am a twin and I suspect I didn't even want to be alone in the womb. Accepting the loneliness was hard, but my teacher insisted I stay with it. As I explored the loneliness, I found an insecurity and a needy kind of emptiness. I remembered these feelings from my early childhood. Much of my sexual desire was an unconscious attempt to fill the emptiness and loneliness. When I held these feelings with compassion, the loneliness began to subside.* Other great thinkers and poets, who I encountered in my years of pointed study, ushered in a way to value and use this loneliness. *Don't surrender your loneliness so quickly, let it cut more deeply, let it ferment and season you as few human or divine ingredients can – Hafez.*

My dance with loneliness is a work in progress. When only a few credits short of graduation from the University of Wisconsin in Madison, in 1971, though hardly conscious of the full parameters of being alone in this world, I grasped the liberation of it. I left in the summer of 1970 for Europe with a friend, Alice. It was an escape trip as the Madison campus was lit up with protest energy against the the U.S. involvement in Vietnam. As an English and Photography major, I spent hours in the darkroom in the Van Vleck Fine Arts building. One evening after leaving the building, it was bombed, and I nearly missed being injured or killed in that event.

The energy of protest, including the justified and expressed anger, took its toll on me that year and the near miss tipped the scales. I wanted a break and Alice was going to Copenhagen to visit extended family there. I took the opportunity and accompanied her. How money was handed out in our family remains erratic; at the time, I must have somehow wrangled enough out of my parents to pay for the flight and travel for the summer. After a stint in Copenhagen with Alice, I returned to Amsterdam and hung out in the youth hostel until the VW bug I had ordered to be in compliance with U.S. exhaust specifications was ready to be picked up. During the wait, I hitchhiked around Europe and England with a few girls I had met in the hostel. Like my first night at Boston College in my single dorm room in Newton, Massachusetts, I knew I was on a new frontier of adventure and self-discovery. As before, this readiness was accompanied by questions and a sense of freedom I could barely manage. The edginess of being alone, truly alone, in an unknown place and part of the world was both exciting and daunting. Whatever reservations I may have had did not hold me back; I dove into situations I might cringe at today like hitchhiking with one of my hostel friends and catching a ride in a 16 wheeler with some guy heading about 135 miles from London to Bristol in the south of England. What I came to know is though I felt "other" in my family, I was still relatively held by the net of family. Each time I stepped further from that nexus, I entered true existential loneliness – by some considered a profoundly adolescent and essential stage of development. This free fall brought with it a renewed urgency to continue to develop the tools to support freedom. Friedrich Nietzsche captures what I experienced then: *It is the business of the very few to be independent; it is a privilege of the strong....He who has attained intellectual emancipation to any extent cannot, for a long time, regard himself otherwise than as a wanderer on the face of the earth and not even as a traveller towards a final goal, for there is no such thing.*

The fabric of my character, the loneliness I had lived and cherished most of the time, met up with something important in the single dorm bed at Boston College and the youth hostel in Amsterdam. Now I was being asked to engage my hard-earned, steely separateness as a survival skill. I learned the ways in which my childhood prepared me for this leap and brought me to a second childhood of sorts where I filled in the holes. Here, during my nearly seven years in Europe, I forged and composed the free wheeling life of an artist, which on a certain level I had always longed for and have longed for ever since. Most significantly, I met my *real* mother in Austria filling in even more holes. Both my foray into living the life of an artist and meeting Frau Engels, my chosen artist mother, had huge significance and life-changing impact. I was now living my way in a world I chose and co-created – a world governed by aesthetic and creative sensibilities – one in which I belonged and was understood and cherished. During my years in Austria, I wrote and photographed daily; I lived a hand-to-mouth existence which, since I had no responsibilities beyond myself, I could afford. This simple, satisfying, soulful life fed me then, and I remain tempted by the freedom-muse to this day.

After traipsing around Holland and England, the VW bug was ready to go. I picked it up – a begged for, premature college graduation present from my parents and joined with some gas-paying girls from the youth hostel to widen the circle of travel. It's unclear in my memory just how I got a graduation gift without having graduated but, either Pat or Joe ended up with the baby blue Ford the three of us shared during the college years. In some households, ending up with a diploma and some wheels was standard before entering the fray of a working life. Maybe Dad's love of cars and travel played a role? Within a few weeks, we drove into Salzburg, Austria, and I fell in love with the place the way you fall in love with a person: hard, irrationally, ecstatically. The copper-roofed buildings surrounding the Salzach river and the looming presence of the Austrian Alps, especially the Untersberg, pulled me in. My magnet was strong and the pull was ferocious. In retrospect, I wonder again about fate and whatever life-design had brought me to this point, as this chapter in my life was utterly essential and gorgeously rich.

My travel companions peeled off in various directions, and I was alone in a boarding house with a one-month commitment. This lowered the price a bit and gave me time to get my bearings. I didn't speak a word of German though my twelve years of Latin came in handy. I had studied Latin and Spanish in high school, but dropped all foreign language studies after that. I guess American isolationist mentality informs the lack of foreign language proficiency as part of the college curriculum. Church Latin for grade school and middle school, then high school level Latin for four years came in handy at this point in my life in ways I could have never imagined. In both my current career as an educational therapist and my life as a writer, my command of language and grammar serves me well. Again, my musings about fate and design rise up as I consider how the various pieces of my studies wove together and supported me at this and many other times in my life. In hindsight, it is easy to see how things braid together to make you who you become.

So, I grabbed my command of English, my journal, and my cherished 35-mm Nikon camera and made a life of it. The first few months in Salzburg were self-directed tourism at its best. I discovered many spots and had plenty of time to reflect and write and photograph, which I did. Chief among the treasured finds was the *KuchenStube* (kitchen room) in the Café Tomaselli. After wandering around for hours in the early morning, I would end up there for my strong black coffee with whipped cream – an *Einspanner* – and a pastry. In the *Stube,* the price for this exquisite breakfast was a tad less than in the elegant rooms of the Café, which faced the *Alter Markt*. As a result, many artists and working class people without much money also frequented this stuffy room near the kitchen, where high-backed wooden booths created privacy and the right to linger longer than one might in the fancy room up front.

This foray into the coffee/cafe culture also had an uncanny relevance to my future. In 1977, I returned to the U.S. and Madison to complete my BA degree in English and Photography. Once done, I tested for and received a BA in German and then did more coursework to acquire a BS in Education in both English and German. I had grown tired of the hand-to-mouth existence of an artist. My intention was to return to Salzburg and teach at the high school level – a "real" job. I also had a boyfriend, Mario, who painted and played the saxophone, which was a minor draw. After the return to college though, I learned I hated teaching, had broken up with the boyfriend, and said yes to an opportunity to go into business with my dentist, who owned a well located building on State Street in Madison. To earn some money during my second college stint, I had babysat for my dentist's children and had given him private photography lessons. He proposed a joint venture on the second floor of his well-located building on State Street

– a photography gallery.

I thought it over and suggested that we open a photography school and gallery inside a European cafe. He was nonplussed as the investment suddenly rose by many thousand dollars, so he backed off temporarily. Furthermore, where was I going to get my share of the money? So I called my dearest brother, Ed, my visionary business guru and lifetime champion to discuss my dream. He was enchanted! In 1977 there was no coffee/cafe culture in the United States, and the concept of photography as art was just blooming. It felt like a dynamic, cutting-edge idea, and a way to integrate my recent experience into my now United States-bound life. He coached and encouraged me to go to the bank and tell them what I had told him. I wavered in a stew of self-doubt for a day or so, then put on my very best attire and walked into the bank. I rolled out my idea, counting on my partner's change of heart, and they loaned me the money requiring a co-signature, which Ed did for me. I couldn't believe it! I was 28 years old with no business degree or experience and, bonanza, I was off and running! Most importantly, I had three successful business men – dentist, brother, and banker, who believed in me.

Dr. Kaplan and I took a third partner, a Swiss woman in the midst of a terrible divorce. She was a great baker and though I had learned from the nephew of the Café Tomaselli to bake as well, I had a bigger task ahead of me in running the business and setting up the photography school and gallery. Sunprint Gallery had two public rooms, a kitchen and a back storage room where the darkroom and teaching table were set up. The name Sunprint came from what Native Americans called photographs as their print method was a contact print using sunlight for exposure. Though steeped in Europe, I was now on American soil. In choosing the name, I looked back on how photography was used and received here and how photographic printing was originally a solar process, using sunlight as a developing and fixative agent. Long before darkrooms and the use of silver, the Mayans and other indigenous peoples used a form of sun printing. The name was apt.

The front end of the space was decorated like a black and white photo – white walls and black, ironlike cafe tables and chairs. The carpet was charcoal and the lighting was directed toward the photography exhibits on the walls. We opened at 7 a.m. with bran muffins and strong coffee hissing out of the dazzling, red-enameled Spanish espresso machine. We initially stayed open until 5 p.m. trying to capture the lunch and the afternoon buzz-seeking crowd with our *Linzertorte, Engadiner Nusstorte* and *Gâteau au Chocolat*. The *Einspinner* or double espresso with whipped cream was featured as well. For lunch, I leaned on my Middle Eastern knack for tabouli, hummus and baba ghanoush in pita bread. There were salads along with a daily soup and quiche special. Photographers were just beginning to have one-person exhibits in some of the fancier galleries in New York in the late 70s. I courted the photographers I admired from afar like Mexican photographer, Manuel Alvarez Bravo, American, Imogen Cunningham, and French photographers Eduard Boubat and Jeanloup Sieff. By writing formal letters, I offered them an opportunity to exhibit their work at Sunprint Gallery. Their hunger and my enthusiasm opened many doors. I promised the purchase of at least two images, some of which make up my personal collection. My role as principal was to oversee the menu, exhibits, hiring and all major financial and aesthetic decisions. After marrying and moving to Vermont, I leased Sunprint for one year before selling it to the lessee. The business still exists but now under a new name, and I bought my Vulcan commercial stove from the money I got in the sale. Just last year in the fine arts museum in Mexico City, my daughters saw a Sunprint Gallery poster featuring Manuel Alvarez Bravo's photo of the merry-go-round horse.

Initially motherless and then finding my *real* mother in Austria in my early 20s is no accident. Was it predetermined? The reincarnation theory of picking your parents comforts me some. It says: you're no victim, but rather you chose this ride-of-a-life to further your development and burn off karma. This idea gives everyone agency even if we don't fully understand it, and I am no exception. If I squint, I can see it all – the misty plan and the execution. The world around me helped too…in fourth grade, at Mary Lou Walsh's house, I saw a large, nine-cat-lap of a woman and her husband in a wheel chair. There were crossword puzzles and Beethoven, but to my mind the calmness was stifling and lifeless. Later, I saw the married lives of my older siblings with dirty cars and oodles of children; I didn't want that either. Two of them had seven children…not for me! I was a wanderer, an independent soul, not fond of being told what to do or how to do it. This could have been the result of being disappointed by the lack of parenting I received, or was the absence of authority and inadequate mother the plan and the teacher? The plan idea explains how I learned to mother myself and the fervent mastery energy I brought to the table early on. I buy it!

There are gifts to being motherless, mostly the survivor's independence. In Austria, I had the opportunity to have a second childhood, and I took it. There I was writing daily in my journal in the Café Tomeselli's *kuchenstube*. Over time, I was invited to join a table of young men, more or less my own age. Martin Flatz and Peter Engels were among them and they figured prominently in the many extraordinary things that spun out for me while in Salzburg. Each of them invited me to meet their parents as they both lived at home still, more customary in Europe than in the United States. Martin's father was Austrian and a prominent member of the equivalent of our planning commission to protect historical properties. He was no longer alive when I came along, but the 11th century *Schloss* (castle) at St. Jakob am Thurn where Martin lived with his mother served as his outstanding legacy. Prunella, Martin's mother, was English and allowed me to live there temporarily if I agreed to bake for and serve tea every day in the garden or the living room depending on the weather. Martin convinced his mother on my behalf, I am sure. I was an avid baker and was running out of money. I did not yet have the photography and tutoring gigs that would eventually sustain me. So I lived in this tower with a mother and son, who weirdly shared bath water and hours of reading, drawing and walking. Let me clarify about the bath water. Only one room in the tower was heated by the beehive *kackelofen*, which was where we spent most days and evenings in winter. The rest of the castle was stone cold and getting hot bath water was a feat. So Prunella would take her bath first and the water was reused by Martin for his weekly bath: weird but practical. As a romantic, I harbored a vague fantasy that Martin and I would marry and live at St. Jakob am Thurn together for the remainder of our days. I performed my job well enough and Prunella enjoyed my company sufficiently, so this arrangement lasted for about six months. My camera was humming, my journal was flooded with impressions, and I was wide-eyed and full of adventure. I remember sitting and writing in the window well, deep enough in the 11th century to hold artists, children, men and women, me, and deep enough to sort of keep out the cold. Next, I was invited to lunch by Peter Engels to meet his mother, Lisl and his father, Erich Engels. I was no longer spending my afternoons in the Café Tomaselli, but my VW bug gave me the flexibility to go into town as needed. Meeting Frau Engels, a revered Austrian painter, cannot be overestimated; it was one of the most significant events of my life. She became my mother. She undoubtedly spared me from some inevitable future psychological disquiet and at least partially healed me of my motherless plight. She saw my beauty, taught me German, modeled how to ski and forage, told me bedtime stories based on the Greek myths, and taught me to garden. She was everything

I ever wanted, and the whim of fate graced my life once again.

For her part, Frau Engels was thrilled to have a daughter, especially someone eager to love a mother, and who sojourned with her in the mountains and the museums she loved. She was probably 54 years old at the time and lived in a gorgeous house across the pond from the famous *Schloss Leopoldskron*, which was and is still owned by the Salzburg Global Seminar. Many exciting artists and thinkers visited here, and Frau Engels' status as a prestigious, female painter drew many of them into her drawing room. She painted mostly landscapes with a feverish stroke. Her trees and mountains shiver and pop with energy. Her palate is ochre, purple, blue, green and golden yellow. Erich, her husband, was an architect who specialized in Gothic restoration. This home and another in a mountain village called *Hintertal*, could have been museums as could Frau Engels' future farm house in *Fuschlsee*. These homes became my playgrounds, my teachers, and my solace; I can see an echo of their old-world charm in my home.

What is it in a home that brings about a hunkering down of the spirit, a soulful plunge into the interior? I lived the answer to this question in Austria: the sheer age of the homes I lived in, the beauty imbued with layers of time in the dishes and linens, the bed frames and bathtubs, the gardens, and the kitchens. When I baked for Prunella Flatz, I poured batter into iron skillets and baked poundcake in ceramic loaf pans, materials not much in evidence in today's kitchen. I made bread puddings in fluted clay molds crafted in the 1700's. I mused about who used these baking beauties over centuries, not years or decades. I imagined Prunella with her English appetite for teatime, packing these inherited kitchen items into her trunk and crossing the sea to Austria. I looked at photographs of her parents and grandparents and knew, instantly, that it was the kitchen staff who had touched and washed these pans and molds. I was the kitchen staff now and relished the role. Isabel Archer in Henry

James' *The Portrait of a Lady* comes to mind again. She is a key person in my life, albeit a fictional character.

As an avid reader in childhood, I took solace from characters on the page as I felt unmet and unseen by the ones in my world. She and others became my friends and mentors. Isabel, the naive American girl in Europe following only the scent of her own ardor, creating a life moment by moment. I love that novel and wanted to name my first born daughter after her, but my then husband vetoed the name Isabel saying it was too English.

My willingness to *go for it* is another characteristic I inherited from my father. Just jump in and trust your essence. Those who can see magic in you, will see it. Work as a plumber and someone will see you're a poet and pull you up. He never said this, but he lived the mantra. He didn't worry about class either. A person is a person no matter what they do, the color of their skin or the lilt of their language. My dad grew up scrapping like all immigrants, and he surely knew and lived the tension among the Irish, Italian and Middle Eastern clans, but this tension never morphed into racism in my father. He worked hard without shame and rose up in the ranks.

The mere mention of him brings up more special experiences together. I remember traveling alone with him to Atlantic City once when I was in my early teens. I don't remember the whys and wherefores of the trip, but my dad loved the casino, the boardwalk, and the smell of the ocean in that town. We bought salt water taffy, rode in a jitney, and met up with his cronies in the town that inspired the names of streets and places in the game of Monopoly. We went there often on vacation, and I relished its old-world feel back in those days. I vividly remember the wooden planks and push carts along with dad's unforgettable friend, Scar, who swam for what seemed like hours in the ocean each morning. Anyway, turns out we were robbed in our hotel, the Traymore, as we slept that night, as were many guests. We realized this when dad noticed his wallet was gone off the bedside table. Luckily, he had two fifties in his pants pocket and when we finished with the reporting of the theft and breakfast, we wandered down to the beach where an African American family with five kids were clearly distraught from having also been robbed that night. My dad went over to the father of the family and gave him one of the fifties, so he could feed his family some breakfast and put gas in their car to get home. He was like that, year-in-and-year-out with anyone who needed a hand. It was automatic in him, a heart reflex. I admire this kind of heart quality beyond all else, and I saw it and felt it as a core quality in my lovable father. Sam Easton valued himself in spite of his lack of an education; he showed up and did what he did best. He was a huckster, polished shoes, drove a taxi, and bootlegged illegal booze until he got married. When he owned his own lumber business, he hired workers and laborers, who 50 years later stood by his grave and wept. He turned plumbers into poets if he needed one with the snap of his fat fingers.

Dad viewed hospitals as spas and checked himself in annually for his "checkup." A veritable storyteller, tipper and charmer, the nurses gave him rub downs with rubbing alcohol, cut his toenails, and changed TV channels before the age of remotes. Nurse to masseuse like plumber to poet, *et voilà*! When he checked out, they hated to see him go. He was robust and healthy until his heart gave out. He died at 93 years old of congestive heart failure, in Jacksonville, on November 2nd, 1999: All Souls Day. Granted, he had ostensibly had a heart attack in his 50s and had open-heart surgery when he was 86 years old but otherwise his health and energy were spectacular. The surgery bought him eight good years. I went to Jacksonville to be next to him when he underwent open-heart surgery; he was terrified and childlike. Maybe I come by my medical anxiety honestly? As robust and lively as he was, he feared many things: mice, heights, snakes, nursing homes and *wasaps* (wasps). When he woke up from the anesthesia in the recovery room, in the midst of ten other drooling and compromised post-operatives, he was sure he had been put in a nursing home. He cursed my mother and ranted to reverse his fate. I sat on his bedside and reassured him we would never let such a thing happen to him – never ever! I can still see the fear in his eyes and hear the bewilderment in his complaints – no doubt the drug hangover escalated his emotions.

In those remaining eight years, he traveled to Italy, bought real estate, and slowly began to grow remote and ready, unconsciously, to move on. My last memory of my father is in the driveway of my home. He and my mother had come for a visit in the summer of 1999. They slept in the living room on my futon as dad couldn't easily do the stairs anymore. I was a working single mother and had to leave for work each morning. I bought a coffee maker with a timer just for him because I couldn't be there to make coffee for him. I had also baked a few loaves of zucchini bread with walnuts, his favorite, and he praised me with every bite. On the day of his departure back to Florida, I came downstairs to see he and my mother spooning. They had mellowed and were living together again after a few year hiatus. He left that afternoon, and we said goodbye, unceremoniously, in the driveway.

Dad's distrust of institutions and his deep regard for the people he loved, brings up another one of his acts of generosity and love. We had five bedrooms and three bathrooms in our stone house in Upper St. Clair. We also had a full basement with a walk-in cedar closet, a washer and dryer and other mechanical things like the furnace and the hot water heater. The basement was rather dark most of the time. A six-foot-plus black man without any known family lived in our basement for most of my childhood. George Cox became a member of our family. He had legendary strength and had worked for many years for my dad. Aging out of his capacity and debilitated by drink, he had nowhere to go but Mayview – yep, that dreaded place where my maternal grandfather lived and died. My father feared all such institutions and, out of the goodness of his capacious heart, wouldn't let this happen to George.

George was a wild and wonderfully picturesque character; he could lift our 1952 black Cadillac up by the front fender, mow the lawn in a jiffy, and dump us gently off the back of the dump truck into tall grass. He ate dinner in the red-and-yellow leather-and-formica kitchen booth in spite of being invited every night by my father to the dining room table with us. "No thank you," he'd say. "Thank the Lord and bless the cook." We kids often joined him in that niche, which had a large mirrored door leading up to the attic area. I remember enjoying our reflection, a gaggle of kids and George, all of us laughing and horsing around. (A far better image-memory than the one in triptych some years earlier). George had the DTs and with it an edge of paranoia and freakiness. I swear I saw him peeking in my bedroom window one night and, on another night, when I went to the basement to get my laundry out of the dryer, he fell to his knees praising me as "The Virgin Mary." I did have a towel around my freshly washed hair, but clearly he was mixing metaphors. The Virgin Mary I learned about did not wear a turban. I was a young adolescent girl, and he was probably a 70-plus year old, delusional, drunk man.

I ran like wildfire up the stairs. I want to trust that my father knew the risks and benefits of giving George a home or he wouldn't have done it. He acted on the knowledge that George would have aged and ended up dying without a loving person in sight, which sadly he did anyway as, after seven to ten years, he wandered off one day never to be seen again. As a loyal and longstanding employee of the Easton Lumber Company, George knew he was guaranteed a home with us for as long as he wanted it.

Another basement memory I have was that of Dorothy Washington, who helped my mother with the laundry and housework. We had a mangle to iron the sheets and table cloths, and I remember sitting on Dorothy's robust lap, my head against her ample breasts and my small white hand on top of her large black hand, with blue or purple-painted, long fingernails, guiding the sheets through the steel rollers of the machine. I loved the smell and heat of the laundry steam that rose up and the closeness of Dorothy's body. Maybe she and George had a thing going on down in the basement, I'm not sure. But she was a sexy, full bodied, big-laughing woman who kept many of us kids entertained with her sexy stories. Sometimes George would be tinkering with something in the basement, and I could see and feel the energy going back and forth between them as the pitch of their stories and laughter rose: another set of parents.

Though my father was a risk taker in business, he took no risks with his daughters. He made this clear. Once Pat and I went into Pittsburgh to shop, and a man squeezed himself in behind Pat and groped her in the rotating glass doors exiting Kaufman's Department Store. We told Dad when we got home, and he launched into a dramatic demonstration of how to kick a man in the balls. Dad was a fireplug of a man, stout and strong, and I can still see him grabbing and kicking with his knee while narrating how to put disgust and anger into the kick. It took a herculean effort to keep him from going to find the guy. He made me laugh so hard I fold in half just thinking about that kick-'em-in-the-balls demo and the time he dressed up for Halloween. Things were winding down, it was late that cold October night and the stream of trick-or-treaters had dwindled down to nothing. Some straggler rang the doorbell, and we opened it to a strangely large kid with a wig, lipstick, high heels and a girdle complete with garter belt with metal clips and stockings. I had no idea it was Dad at first. He had gone out the back door and come up the front steps. The getup was that unfortunate fleshy-peachy-pink color, and I can still see him unable to keep the secret when we kids stared at him in disbelief. His laugh was unmistakable and contagious and gave away his identity. He had a way of breaking through his persona, which was both remarkable and admirable; above all, he knew who he was and was comfortable in his own skin. He was a guy's guy, no doubt, but that he would dress up as a woman shows his knack for bending the boundaries.

Dad was predictable, his thoughts and actions consistent with the patriarchy of his generation and ethnicity, but he was also deeply human and alive, so he broke the mold just as often. My sister Pat often expresses having been afraid of Dad and experienced his unpredictability as frightening. I had a very different response, even to his temper, as he was transparent and easily readable to me. I could see what made him tick. He was a madly successful business man because of his savvy, his people skills, his immigrant need to succeed, and the love and respect he won with his humanitarian heart and his willingness to laugh.

Among the many high school experiences that fits into the magic and racial education my dad gave me was going to see Cassius Clay fight against Charley Powell in the Civic Arena in the winter of 1963 in Pittsburgh. Why did I go alone with Dad and none of the other kids accompanied us? I have no idea except I was game for that sort of thing. It was a stormy, snowy night in January, and we crept through the drifts and traffic to get downtown; we lived about 16 miles south of Pittsburgh. Dad pulled right up front of the Civic arena, per usual for him at airports and hotels, and someone got a ten or a twenty to park the car. The cop got a wink and maybe a twenty buried in the hand shake. Dad had a long-standing relationship with the cops perhaps stemming from his bootlegging days. He knew how to get around. We walked through the electric crowd and my dad was greeted over and over again: "Sam, Sam, Sam Easton." We waded down through the crowd to our ringside seats. My father had connections in Pittsburgh and was probably betting heavily on the fight.

I was in every possible minority category in the arena that night: race, gender and age. But I remember feeling proud to be his daughter, to be in the heat of the moment, and to be visible. I walked behind him and was swept up in the wake of his presence and the royal reception he received always and everywhere. We slid onto the bleachers and the crowd quieted down as Muhammad Ali, still called Cassius Clay, came out in his robe. His trainer stood behind him and slipped the satin robe off his shoulders when he was introduced. WOW, from then on...

Ali was 21; I was 14. He dazzled me with the lightning movement of his white satin shorts, by his confidence and power, his footwork and dancer's flight, and by his muscled chest sparkling silver and bronze with sweat. I had never seen a practically naked man and what an introduction: apologies to every naked man I've seen since, but Ali is a hard act to follow. I stepped into the world of men that night and into Dad's kind of school – I was wide-eyed and rapt and liked this school even more than high school. My radar antenna were wiggling and reaching in all directions. Just being in a crowd that size, that color, that revved and focused, opened new energy channels in me. The presence of such a great figure like Ali helped me manage this burst of energy. He embodied grace and mastery, beauty and intensity. Despite the strangeness of my circumstances – a young, white girl ringside at the fight – I felt at home and in awe.

It is interesting that I had no negative response to the blood and gore of the fight. I hate that kind of thing now and cannot make it through violent movies. Boxing is not a sport I watch or admire. But this was different; Ali was the protagonist who I fell in love with and every punch he took made me root for him even more. I was in the experience and didn't smell the blood. I identified with him, as I am a fighter too in my own right.

Back to my father's story, he had to quit school at the end of third grade to help earn a living for his family. His father had taken sick and there was no choice. Nigibi expected help from her children, and she got it life-long from my father. Sister Bernadette, who took a shine to this little man, held dad's hand and helped explain why he had to stop coming to school. In fact, he entered a new kind of school. He got out there on the street and learned about life by looking, doing, and being in many situations that must have often been way over his head.

Being in the arena that night was over my head, too. I conjecture that on some level my father knew that all his kids, even his girls, had to learn from the school of life sooner or later. He defended this kind of education many times like when my sister Pat skipped school and had to be ushered back in by a parent. My dad went with her as it must have been a Friday morning, and he had just returned from his weekly poker game with corned beef, bagels, tootsie rolls and a five-o'clock shadow. I loved Friday mornings because he woke us up the minute he got in the house at around 6:00 a.m. with the rich smell of food and a humorous, woozy and unshaven smile. After savoring this tasty breakfast, we got to play a round of Crazy Eights before going to school. Dad's mood was not affected by winning or losing. He loved his poker games and his poker friends and held on to this pleasure well into his 90s, amazing his children with his stamina for the all-nighters.

On that one morning when he went in to see the principal with Pat in his unshaven state and heard that not only had Pat skipped school, but she had jumped over the fence to leave the premises. Dad said, "Yeah – all of my kids are *ath a letic* and, you know, there is a lot to learn out there even when you're not in school." He went on to talk about himself and how he left school young and took up in its place the school of hard knocks. The principal was nonplussed.

Sometimes I think that my sister Pat and I "job shared" in childhood. That is, she was funny where I was serious; she was a magnet for boys, and I was a geek; she was naughty while I was a "goody-two-shoes;" she was shy but wildly extroverted, and I was not shy but wildly introverted. She put me up to a few unforgettable pranks, the most memorable of which was making and serving my father "poo stew" in her response to his annoying demands to be waited on. We put dog poop, cut grass, and warm water into a wide soup bowl and served it up. Dad was understandably furious! I had been played, which happened often as one of the youngest.

Pat and I are very different yet remain close as adults. We share memories of our family mythology as we grew up more or less at the same time. She is two-and-a-half years my senior. I often do fact checking with her and compare notes, but she is one of my mother's favorites, so our perception of the family gestalt is vastly disparate. She grew up afraid of Dad, yet she pushed his buttons not caring if he was mad and, like my mother, pretending to ignore him when he got intense. Pat talks about deciding to be "the funny one" because all other categories were taken by her brothers and sisters: athletic, beautiful, creative, smart, etc. My character formed from the inside out, the idea of constructing an identity is foreign to me. Currently, Pat's role in our family as mediator and comedian has caused some tensions between us. I am a straight shooter and say what I mean as often as possible. Pat may say one thing to me and then turn it upside down to stay on the good side of her listener. The most recent example of this is about writing this memoir. To me she says how great it is that I am writing daily, and she is in full support of my efforts. A week later, she says to my brother Ed, "I am glad my last name isn't Easton, who knows what might come out in JoAnna's memoir." Feeling unsafe and critical of this sort of split-tongued hypocrisy, I hold her accountable and then distance myself until I recover.

I remember another one of dad's gutsy moves when we were driving to Florida in the 1952 Cadillac with its huge wheel wells where I slept: no seat belts in those days. We were driving through Georgia at night, and I woke up to dad's cursing lament, "Dammit, you always get pinched in Georgia." We were getting pulled over for speeding, and my dad wasn't going to play nice. However, these were not Pittsburgh cops! He was lavish with money when gambling or buying a new ride, but unwilling to waste it on a speeding ticket – I can relate. There were six kids in the car and my mother, and when the cop was done posturing, he tells my dad to pay the ticket of $250; Dad flatly refused. "If you don't pay the ticket, you'll have to spend the night in jail," the cop countered. My dad, unafraid of police, called his bluff and said, "Okay, it's late. We're all tired, and it's cheaper than a hotel for eight of us." Screaming from the back seat, I begged not to go to jail. Dad would not back down though, and soon we were moving down some lonely dark road in Georgia on our way to jail with the cop car and shrill blue lights in escort. At the entrance, we had to be separated: boys with men, girls with women. I remember feeling more panic; I wanted to go with my father where I felt safe. He was someone you knew could get you out of a tight spot if necessary. My mother exuded no such confidence. No way would Dad let this bossy cop win that match and, on some level, I knew he had the upper hand. I may have inherited my flagrant disregard for authority from him too.

As headstrong and self-possessed as was my father, I called upon my own reserves of confidence throughout my life. With some of his verve, as I like to think of it, I made my way through Austria, baking pound cake and French *Tarte Tatin* and tutoring a brood of kids with a smile on my face. This was in my blood and in my soul along with the abundant energy I also inherited from Dad. In Europe, I was back in the land of apples and navigating with the powerful compass of the seventh child: curious, intuitive and determined. Little did I know, I was about to surrender to my second childhood. Lunch that day at Frau Engels' table consisted of veal cutlets and mountain cranberries called lingonberries. (Though I was a vegetarian, I was eating meat for a short stint, as vegetarianism didn't work without a steady income and a regular kitchen of my own.) The veal had sage leaves fried in sweet butter on top, a signature dish of Frau Engels. Lunch was the big meal of the day, and she went all out for me, her eventual *Haustochter* (house daughter). Our fate was sealed. She had a dying father, a cheating husband, and two self-absorbed sons, but she possessed the whimsy, drive and independence of an artist. She was a mimosa in a man's world. Frau Engels had no driver's license and several, already scheduled, one-person art exhibits scattered all over Austria. Erich was tired of schlepping her around, and her sons were disengaged. I showed up and filled as many needs in her life as she did in mine. I was a girl! Additionally, I had a deep urge to have a mother, had a VW bug, and no steady job or responsibilities. It was a fit, two puzzle pieces sliding into place with that familiar magnetic click. *Engel* in German translates to angel in English! Here she was – my *motherangel* – and from her point of view, I was the sunrise in the east.

Her life could be a book, but how it entwined with mine remains as magical and mysterious as the sudden rise of mist and avalanches. With her, I visited every corner of Austria and stayed on the estates of the most royal art patrons in the country. She taught me German along the way, gave me a tour of the most well known churches, narcissus fields, and castles. We ate well, traveled widely, and later renovated a farm house on Atterseee together where I think she was already "shopping" for her next home. I learned that planting and watering nasturtiums near a slaked lime, whitewashed wall was ideal, and that planting and digging, steaming and eating new potatoes made for the finest meal ever with a fair share of sweet butter and fresh parsley leaves, of course. I still plant nasturtiums every year and cannot imagine my garden without them and without her. Gardening holds the elements of stillness and bonding to nature and to her. Like my sweet mother, I live for contemplation and participation in the majesty of nature as this is my bridge to creativity as it was for her.

Upon Seeing the Lotus

The green is ethereal
on the lotus leaf,
the viscosity of water
is held in beadlets –
mercury-like in the concave center
where the water intrigues me further
with its cold, wild color of ice.

In this state of exquisite oneness
I am the ravenously red hollyhock.
I am the Buddha's lotus leaf.
I am even the bulbous frog
with a chartreuse face
trumpeting out with throaty joy.

Virginia, the tiger cat comes near,
she paws the water beneath the lotus leaf,
shaking the stunned frog –
Everything begins to shimmer and move
in response to her inquiry.

Thyme lay in full bloom, round and about
the tiny pond, and…in stillness
I am reminded of the other time,
the grabbing of it,
the surrendering to it
in order to invite reverie –
and am pleased to remember
I know about Thyme and time.

Frau Engels lived and breathed as an artist, but I didn't learn her fine art of neglecting housework and children for the sake of art, every day and always, but I'm working on it. She was a mediocre mother to her own sons while being a perfect mother to me, a 21 year old American girl hungry for love, art, and beauty. Her priorities were clear and focused. She wasted little time fretting over relationships and domestic imperfections and got into her studio, nature, the mountains and her garden to feed her art. She had lived through World War II in hiding with her sons in the mountains where food was scarce. When cooking with an egg, she wiped out the inner shells with her fingers, wasting nothing. She knew how to forage for mushrooms, blueberries, lingonberries, and make an Italian gelato out of scraped glacier ice, lemon juice, zest and sugar. Her father brought her into the *AlpenVerein*, a hiking and climbing club, where she climbed every prominent mountain in Austria with him as a young woman. Her father saw the artist in her and paid for her to go to a famous art school in Vienna instead of regular school. She, too, had a good father.

We spent many weeks at a time in the mountains, ate bread with cardamon and sweet butter and in the company of farmers and sheepherders on the *hochalm* (high pastures) above Hinterthal. Once I was chased by a wild boar; Frau Engels watched me running and screaming in genuine fear, but it hit her funny bone. She surmised I was in no mortal danger and delighted in the vibrant energy of the moment. Paralyzed with laughter, she was doubled over and clapping her hands in glee. So much transpired in these moments together. She delighted in my readiness to embrace life and also saw my innocence and fears. I laughed at myself through her eyes, a laugh of tender love for her and for me. She and I hiked up mountain sides with seal skins and turned to ski back down. First we would rest by eating our lunch with our noses in the sun on some porch of an abandoned hut. We wrapped the skins around our waists and skied back down to the her house in the valley below. In summer, we picked narcissus, gathered mushrooms and dunked in icy river water. I have dozens of pictures of myself in those fields and rivers because she took them, got them printed, and pressed them into my hands. She knew what bloomed when and where and, in addition to traipsing around Austrian towns to set up her art exhibits, we followed what was ripening and bursting into fullness in the mountains and valleys she knew and loved. Why did I end up in Austria? Like Elizabeth Barrett Browning, in Sonnet 43: *How do I love thee? / Let me count the ways / I love thee to the depth and breadth and height /My soul can reach, when feeling out of sight / For the ends of being and ideal grace.*

Let me count the ways. The mountains were the first clue; other than Wisconsin, I had always lived near and been drawn to mountains. The uneven horizon that mountains create, with the pockets of ground fog in the valleys that burn off in the morning sun, matches the curves and dips in my psyche. A flat horizon seems impoverished by comparison. Meeting Frau Engels and living a redeeming second childhood figures as the love and fate factor that drew me to Salzburg. The Baroque copper roofs and artistic vibe of Salzburg felt like a match. Austria values art and its artists and provides some of them with a stipend and a state-financed atelier space. The Mozarteum Salzburg founded in 1841, is a famous university with a focus on music and the dramatic arts. The art vibe was more than a vibe for me as it offered me my first job as a photographer and introduced me to the opera, which reacquainted me with my love of music and language. Though foreign, I understood what was being sung. It felt like the lessons learned from my dad, who exposed me to reading the emotive lilt of language, faces and character. At the feet of his mother, I learned to stand in the rain of foreign language music. I let the words pour down on me and after a while, I found my way into the pauses and the passion: the syntax behind literal understanding. This is how I learned German and how I felt at home listening to Verdi's *La Traviata* in Italian or Wagner's *Ring* in the magnificent *Festspielhaus*, Salzburg's festival venue designed by architect Clemens Holzmeister, with Frau Engels long before I was fluent in German. In Salzburg, I landed my first photography job at the *Mozarteum* photographing opera singers, violinists and actors.

The Universität Mozarteum Salzburg, founded in 1841 to commemorate the 50th anniversary of the death of Wolfgang Amadeus Mozart, is a university specializing in music and the dramatic arts. I was hired to create portfolios for graduating performing artists. Again, pure luck, connections and timing as, at that time in the early 1970s, the 35 mm camera had not yet taken hold in Europe; most photographers had studios and large format, cumbersome 4X5 Hasselblads and Leicas. These are magnificent instruments – I wish I owned one – but it was my 35 mm Nikon with its mobility that got me the job in Salzburg because I could go to the school stage, piggyback on stage lighting and get up under the arm of a violinist or practically in the mouth of an opera singer. By now I had my own apartment on the Getreidegasse, owned an enlarger, a few developing trays and had set up a darkroom in my bathroom. I was quick, skilled, eager and broke – nothing like that combination to foster a spirit of flexibility and service. I met some real characters too. I particularly remember a Rubenesque beauty named Marilyn. She was an American, who had lived and studied opera in Italy and now in Salzburg. After spending an afternoon photographing her, we had dinner. For the following year, we would meet from time to time, and she kept me entertained and got me laughing hysterically over the ways she sought and found the sex she claimed to need before she sang: "Works wonders on my voice, keeps my throat lubricated and relaxes me in important ways. I can't sing well without it." That played right into a script of my Dad's that sex was necessary and Marilyn was a case in point. She was graphic and experienced, and I loved her mezzo-soprano voice and her stories revealing the sperm-based secrets of her success. She reveled in the telling, was successful, and I think of her and laugh when I listen to Maria Callas trill up and down the scale until, with a shiver, I let go into the intense beauty and feeling of her voice.

My artist nature was fully realized during my years in Salzburg. For the one and only time in my life I smoked cigarettes for a few months when I lived alone on the Getriedegasse and developed film and photos into the wee hours of the morning. Per usual, I did it up "right" by smoking the filterless, French, black tobacco of *Gitane* and *Gauloise,* the favorites of Albert Camus and Jean Paul Sartre. I would photograph for several hours at the Mozarteum or the artists' ateliers on the Salzach and then go home, grab a bite to eat, and set up the darkroom. On the same table that now serves as my dining room table, I would lay out the prints, light up a smoke and edit them with satisfaction. I was living the artist's life and relished both the idea and the life itself. That same table that has been dragged along with me all these years was found on a fire pile in the countryside near Attersee outside of Salzburg. The farmer was giving up this beauty for a formica replacement, I suspect, but their loss was my gain. It is a talisman from those years and has remained an important fixture in my life carrying so many memories from the black and white photos of Marilyn and others, to the autobiography I wrote for my poetry writing class with the poets John Engels and Alan Broughton. Fast forward, my babies, friends, lovers and ex-husband have eaten many meals at this table, and often I sit at it alone for a meal or type up this memoir on its smooth, well-worn, nut wood surface. It is curious what arises in a life. Our art? Our spirit? Or does it all come down to a handful of tangible things that get passed along hand-to-hand?

As the years passed and I came back to the States, married and had my beautiful daughters, Frau Engels visited me twice, and I returned twice to Austria in the ten-plus years that separated us. When I returned for her 90th birthday celebration in 2006, an unspeakably tender finale awaited me. She was frail by then though she continued to live alone in the farmhouse in Fuschlsee, which she acquired and gladly retreated to after her husband's death. The snow was up to the eaves on the March day that I arrived by taxi. She came out in her *dirndl* and with a cane to shower me with hugs and kisses. She had moved into the guest room to give me her room and yummy bed as her honored daughter-guest. I didn't want to take her cozy bed. "Please," she insisted. I put my bags down and we went out for a walk, one we had taken many times together when she was still spry. She had not been out for weeks for fear of falling and hooked her right arm in mine. Her cane, in her left hand, poked into the ice. Though changed in many ways since I had seen her last, she experienced signature joy on our evening walk, a pink glow on the mountains ringing the valley lit up her face and eyes. We ate a light meal, caught up a bit, and headed to bed on the early side. On that first night, I was jet lagged and weary. She came into my/her room with her white hair flowing and carrying a hot water bottle to warm the icy bed sheets – ever my mother.

As she sat on the edge of my bed, her bed, I looked up to the bookshelf overhead and noticed five, two inch thick bound volumes with my name and dates on the bindings. *What is this?* One by one, we brought them down onto the feather-bed / duvet, and I turned the pages of our life together immortalized by my beloved mother. "One day I knew we'd sit on my bed, just like this, and you would find these books," she said. The many letters, photographs, postcards and memories had been collected and bound by her. Dumbfounded with emotion, I cried myself to sleep that night. The satisfaction combined with the contrast of having nothing from my first childhood stunned me. The painstaking effort, tenderness and love that went in to such a tribute sealed most of the motherless cracks in my heart. She also gave me a spectacular piece of jewelry her mother had given her: a gold butterfly pin with cobalt blue laminate wings and a diamond body designed by Ernst Faltscho. Mother to daughter – mother to daughter.

Just a few months later, Frau Engels died alone in her farmhouse near the lake. I was in the kitchen when the phone rang. It was the woman who came in with food and cleaned her house for the last ten years. I had given her my contact information while there and when I heard her speaking to me in German, I sank to the floor. I knew why she had called when she said "GrussGott Frau JoAnna." I heard the details of Frau Engels' fall down the stairs hitting her head, and lying there alone for who knows how long. The small plane flying her to the hospital unconscious…and her death. I hung up the phone and wailed in pain. I was dazed, though how could I be surprised? Her doctor visited her while I was in Austria, and she wanted me in the room with them. He explained how she could fall or have a stroke. He felt she should have more support by moving into an assisted living arrangement. She explained that she wanted to die in that house and if she fell, she fell! I think the doctor hoped I would chime in on his behalf, but I knew my mother well and knew she consciously chose to stay in the farmhouse and experience the end of her life there. I could not imagine her anywhere else either! I lay on my kitchen floor and saw her again riding her bike to town with her eyes on the mountains, wiping out egg shells when she cooked, and painting in her studio with the lightness and fierceness of a bird. Just as she died alone on the floor of her foyer, I said goodbye to my mother alone on my kitchen floor, my head on her imaginary shoulder.

Rows and rows of books have been and still are a prominent and precious feature of my life. Frau Engels' scrapbooks were not the first time rows of books have showed up in my life. In fact, the rows of journals that line up on a shelf in my writing and working studio have followed me around from house to house over dozens of years. They hold acres of words and testify to my steadiness and to the underlying questions and patterns that persist in my life.

The first time I remember rows of books being called to my attention was at a visit with my beloved sister, Peggy, to a powerful medium, Grace Brewer, in rural, northern Florida near Georgia. I'm not sure how the idea got hatched, but there we were ringing the bell at the small door of a tiny house across the street from a white church where she was a pastor, non-traditional. When a wizened, petite woman opened the door, I felt a spooky gloss come over me. The whiteness of her – her hair and skin the color of oatmeal – was from too much seeing, I guessed. Peggy and I each had a reading. I had recently married Willy, and we were in the process of deciding on where he would take a professorship job, which dictated where we would live. Her frail body began to rock and vibrate, "I see deep forests and rows of books in your life. Open the books and maybe write in them. Choose trees, not water." She also predicted that I would have two daughters, but I "would have to suffer in bed for them. Do it. You will want to do it." She said my husband would give me an ordinary life but "he will not be the man you hold." She said, "You will die easily when you are ready. You will have next to you a few good women friends, your children, and the man you held." At the close of our meeting she said, "Have secrets but no regrets; you've only taken enough to live on." She repeated rows of books many times in her reading, and I smile each time I see those rows in almost every room of my house. I justify my book addiction by donating hundreds of books to libraries and Good Will each year.

In truth, I had no ordinary life with Willy. We were introduced by my co-English major friend, Ann Moore, in Madison, Wisconsin. By this time, I was running Sunprint Gallery, and

Willy was getting his doctorate in Industrial Engineering. He came in for lunch with Ann in order to meet me. Our first dates were to Werner Herzog and Ingmar Bergman movies on campus. We started seeing each other more, lived together for a few years and later married on May 31,1982. We traveled extensively. Willy got tenure at the University of Vermont, and we have two fabulous daughters. We got divorced in 1996. Our love, on the other hand, could be called ordinary as it lacked the sterling luster of a love that deepens with time and endures the ups and downs of life.

Going to a medium with Peggy is not out of character for us as we share the draw to the mystical. Margaret Mary or Peggy, as she is called, was the first born and the most beautiful and feminine in our family. Her oldest son, Davey, was just four years my junior and, in many ways, was my little brother. Davey discovered his dad's infidelity and was fatally scarred by this experience. He became a drug addict and died of AIDS in 1994 when he was barely 40 years old. This was a huge loss for everyone. He was the first person close to me to become ill and die, and his was the first funeral in our family. Stephen Levine's book *Who Dies?* helped me conceptualize death differently at this time, comforted me and helped me make it through the grieving: *If we take each teaching, each loss, each gain, each fear, each joy as it arises and experience it fully, life becomes workable. We are no longer a "victim of life." And then every experience, even the loss of our dearest one, becomes another opportunity for awakening.* On March 26th I sat on a plane en route to this sad event and wrote the following entry in my journal: For Butterflies and David, Most Especially – *This is a time of profound transformations! For David, most especially, indeed for all f us who stayed present in this process of letting go. We all, at some time in our lives witness the struggle as flesh and spirit work out their relationship. At certain times we sense equilibrium, at others, dominance of either spirit or flesh. Yet always, there is reason to turn our hearts to the moment. In birth, spirit becomes flesh. I imagine "spirit" being caught in a butter-fly net, placed in the womb of a woman to transform and incubate, finally to emerge as flesh. In death, the process is reversed. The flesh diminishes and life is converted back to spirit. We all participate in this alchemy – some reluctantly, some joyfully, some prefer flesh, some seek spirit. On March 25th, 1994 David transformed back to spirit. Oh spirit – what color, what shape of wing?*

The secret of moving from victim status to agency status lies in being fully present and digesting all of life's experiences. At least, this is what I try to live by, and I consider this credo to be my saving grace. Davey's death and funeral, a direct conse-quence of his short life, puts him in the ranks of the lucky ones as he died a personal, non-violent death. The loss reignited my spiritual path, which had been sidelined by the aversion I felt toward Catholicism; its rules, social conservatism, reverence for suffering, and so much else. Yet, as the quasi-mystical experi-ences of my life continued and now in the shadow of Davey's death, I began reading in the Buddhist tradition and started meditating daily and attending group meditation sessions led by a wise and gifted intuitive healer named Don Mercurio. More experiences flowed in. "Waking up" from meditation was hard at first as I had to travel the distance between my daily life and this inner and upper chamber.

To meditate, I sat in an ultra-wide Mission chair, which I inherited from my dear Madison, Wisconsin photographer friend, Mary Allen. She frequented Sunprint Gallery, and we became friends. After her husband died, she was left alone in a rambling farm house in Black Earth, Wisconsin. Each season, an artsy group of friends joined Mary in her working parties where we stacked wood, removed and washed screens, raked leaves, planted tomatoes and harvested apples depending on the season. Mary stayed inside whipping up a splendid country dinner of bean stew and apple crisp, using what was on her land. At a certain point, she had to move, and she let each of the steady, annual helpers pick a favorite piece of art or furniture as a memento of thanks at the last party in that rambling farm house; we were there to help her pack and get ready for the movers. That's now one of the chairs in my office in LittleWing Learning Center, my educational therapist / special education private practice.

In these years, 1994-1996, I baked skinny French bread called *ficelle* (string) and rose before the children and my husband to get it going. This is when I meditated in that chair just as the sun was rising. It's a notably powerful time of day, and I progressed quickly, so I learned to hold onto the vibe while I was carrying out my daily life. I had resigned as a Food Editor for Harrowsmith Magazine at the time and was selling my bread at the Shelburne Supermarket. We had returned from a sabbatical year in Bois Le Rois (forest of the king) east of Paris.

My husband and I had agreed that if I resigned from the work as an editor and joined him on his sabbatical then, upon our return, I could pursue my dream to get an MFA in writing. This was yet another in a long string of unkept promises, one of the straws that eventually broke me. He had been cheating on me since my pregnancy with Amanda, our first born, (or even before for all I know), and I was less and less able to justify staying in the marriage. We fought often, and I succumbed to the same dynamic I saw in my father: sadness underneath and anger on the surface. I had to get out – the echoes of neglect and abuse, lies and broken promises rose to scream in my head and my heart was breaking. During the many years of discontent, I would flirt with men, yet I knew if ever I acted on my rising desires, it would become violent. The double standard was alive and well. In a journal entry around this time I wrote the following about a chance encounter with a handsome workman: *I was once again put in touch with the erotic side of my journey. It is quite clear to me that physicality is a key to what lies inside. Happily, I had experienced freedom and flight in my body athletically and sexually* and had no desire to abandon that part of my journey. The other day, I stopped to say hello to Jim who was mowing a lawn. I was on my bike. We kissed hello as we always do, but I slipped a little in my cleats and fell into his neck. I was surprised and aroused by his smell, the warmth of his skin, the sensation of my mouth on his skin. It was a strange moment – time stopped for a second, and I again experienced and welcomed this expansiveness that I have already described here often. A pleasurable feeling – sensual and soft – a kind of wall-less melting into the other. I love feeling safe enough to let go like that, and it had become rare for me to feel safe and aroused at the same time in my marriage.

On Burdock And Desire

Purple burdock pods bristled and frizzy
erect with leaves, explode
in our meadow within a wind's breath
of the farmer's cow fields and corn fields.

A workman, Jim, came with his brush hog,
downed the stalks and broke the cycle.
He stooped to pitch a stone,
his hip, smooth and tight as a horse flank.
His white and brown Spaniel, Molly,
ran behind him in a path of pressed grasses,
her flannel ears rose and fell.

One summer day, he stood quiet
in the shade of our white porch,
while I gave my breast,
blue-veined and tight-skinned with milk,
to my newborn daughter.

In January, some years later,
when trucks and brush hogs
lay dormant under snow,
I thought of him.
I remembered his blue eyes
on the blue of my breast,
and the weight
of his jacket in my hands
when I lifted it up
from the hood of his truck,
and rubbed my face
near-raw, in its woolliness.

It is summer again.
I stand in that same field,
now full of sunflowers.
He whizzes by in his truck.
Molly's ears flap out his window
rising and falling on air currents,
her dense weight between his legs
her hair parted against his face.

At some point after my first daughter's birth and realizing the frozen, unfulfilled landscape of my marriage, there were moments when I felt myself drift toward other men. One particular event was someone I met at a wedding I attended in Acapulco in March, 1991. Like with Jim, this encounter awakened something in me that had fallen asleep yet, in a matter of seconds, rose fiercely and brought me face-to-face with the magical and delightful part of my nature now in hiding. I stood on the dock by the lagoon and watched as a man named Michel, a competitive water skier, skied the slalom course with perfect grace and intense power. As he finished, he swooshed in, leaned toward the spectators with a wave and smiled in a state of complete happiness. As I saw him, I saw my gymnast-self at the same time. Yes, it was the wave and the smile – a gesture of triumph, showmanship, and satisfaction that grabbed me by the heart.

Over the course of the wedding weekend, I saw Michel many times, danced with him, spoke to him, and drank with him. It was clear that our lives had some parallel lines: moments of magic and delight mixed with other times when we were dark, frightened, angry and tired. I learned from the elders at the wedding that Michel had been treated poorly by his mother, Alice, and would often come as a child to stay at my x's house, as his father, Bernard, and my father-in-law, Dede were good friends. Lucette, my mother-in-law, would hold and bathe this little man and try to ease his body sores. In his childhood, the stepmother, Jacqueline, the hostess of this wedding event, was even less kind to Michel. In short, he suffered deeply in the mother department and "still looks for love." No wonder I could relate to his triumphant smile. We were two of a kind: survivors who had escaped our loveless mothers and found triumph in our physical mastery of a controlled and ecstatic sport.

I wrote to him later in my journal: *From the moment of the wave and the smile, I can only say that meeting you felt like pulling a loose thread on a sweater and watching the whole sleeve unravel in a minute. All of my contact with you was contact with myself. Like the sweater metaphor, it took years to knit defenses and justifications and only minutes for it to unravel. As you skied and my awareness heightened, I remembered myself in gymnastics, my first sport. It was a sport in which flexibility and strength are critical, but timing and concentration, risk-taking, trusting and yielding to the movement itself are essential. I brought all my pain, all my loneliness, and all of my gift to that sport. It was something I could master. It was fair. If I trained hard, I got better and better. A simple and satisfying effort-to-outcome relationship. When I completed a performance and had done well, I smiled with just the same feeling of grounded ecstasy that I felt in your smile. I see you, and I get you!*

From the book *Mapping The Terrain of the Heart: Passion, Tenderness, and the Capacity to Love,* edited by Stephen Goldbart, I read about six capacities of love that are necessary in order to create a stable love relationship: erotic involvement, merging, idealization, integration, "refinding," and self-transcendence. I have experienced all of those capacities in love relationships but often don't find them reciprocated. The desire and capacity to merge a part of oneself with a part of the beloved, like the over-lapping part of a Venn diagram, is largely missing in the men I have loved and was utterly missing in my marriage.

On the subject of men, I have always known that the connection to men would play a significant role in my life. My repetitive dream, my innate response to men, and my interest in tantra, pointed the way. There have been many men through-out many years, some left so little behind that I cannot even remember their names. Others left honeyed sweetness in their wake, and still others left cavernous love-holes and/or scars be-hind; each of these men are forever part of the fabric of who I am. Between the age 17 and 29, and then 45 until now, I have been unmarried. That's quite a few years: 37 to be exact. In those separate spans of time, I lived out my relative beauty and eager sexuality with freedom and joy. Men were attracted to me and I to them. I love men and, as troublesome as they have been at times, I wouldn't trade them for any other love interest. I'm inclined toward handsome, talented, intelligent, gifted, selfish and eccentric men – no wonder the heartaches.

My first realized love occurred in the first two years of my time in Madison at the university. Stephen R. was the editor of the university newspaper, The Daily Cardinal, and a writer. He was from New York city and returned there to work as an editor of a prominent news magazine after graduation. That move ended our relationship, but in the meantime, it was a sweet, live-together arrangement. We even had a dog: a Hungarian pointer, a Vizsla, named Jude after The Beatles "Hey Jude…"

Before I met Stephen in Wisconsin, though, I met Tom M. who became and has remained an important person in my life and in my fantasy life for many reasons. The camera and the bike brought us together. In the summer between Boston College and my transfer to UW, my father, twin brother and I traveled to Japan, Hong Kong and Okinawa to meet up with my brother, Sam, who was serving as a Captain in the Marine Corps in Vietnam. We timed our trip to meet him in Okinawa on his R&R. This was the first time I had traveled outside of the United States, and it was an eye-opener. Sweetly, my brother Sam gave me a gift of a Nikon FM, which he had purchased at the duty-free. This gift changed the course of my university studies and my life in substantial ways. I was 17 years old and aware of my body in a new way. I had had sex with a man, which can change a girl into a woman like it or not! Being on a military base with literally hundreds of men at this stage in my life caused an internal, unfathomable wave. The wave was held back within the walls of the military and the presence of my father and brothers. Outside of that setting, however, I saw no need to hold my erotic tides in check. It was the family, catholicism and immaturity that prevented me from exploring my sexuality until I was out of the house and living on my own.

The camera and the bike, and many other objects serve as historical memorabilia and connecting rods to significant relationships in my life. As I look around my home, I see gifts and feel the presence of many beautiful people who peppered my life with kindness, recognition and love in the dozens of *objets d'art* they gifted to me. I already mentioned the Mission chair, now in my office where I began my meditation practice and nursed my babies dozens of years ago. It has a funky, square shape wide enough for my crossed legs; it is made of iron and wood, strong and hardy materials. The previous owner, Mary Allen, suffered with depression, which worsened after her husband's illness and death. A community of artist friends gathered around her to shore her up as best we could. She had a fabulous photography collection including the Running White Deer piece by Paul Caponigro. Tom M. and I had driven to Chicago to see a photography exhibit at the Museum of Contemporary Art and some of what we saw were among the stunning pieces in Mary's collection. Visiting Mary at her home was also a museum-like experience as she and her husband collected artifacts and photography from their life together in California and on travels. I helped appraise Mary's collection with my dear friend, Paul Vanderbilt, photography archivist at the Historical Society in Madison. That she would give us each something was unexpected and so welcome as she is now with me for all of time in sacred meditation.

On top of my kitchen hut is the oblong wooden bread bowl given to me by Paul Vanderbilt. Once I opened Sunprint Gallery, he was a regular, visiting the cafe daily for a coffee and a treat and viewing the photography exhibits of Manuel Alvarez Bravo, Imogen Cunningham and Edouard Boubat to name a few of the heavy-weight exhibitors. As an archivist for the Federal Security Administration (FSA), Paul remained interested in the role of photography in history – he had the archival impulse. This was written about Paul in "From the Monuments of Men" where 345 men and women are honored for their efforts to save cultural treasures from the destruction of WWII, Hitler and the Nazis: *Shortly before the bombing of Pearl Harbor, Vanderbilt began working as a records coordinator with the U.S. Navy in Washington, D.C. The following year, he was selected by Roy Stryker, head of the Farm Security Administration-U.S. Office of War Information (FSA-OWI) to catalogue the Administration's vast photographic collection. The FSA-OWI began as part of the Resettlement Administration, a New Deal program devoted to relocating thousands of Americans from agriculturally exhausted farmland to newly-formed greenbelt communities. Vanderbilt helped arrange and classify over 200,000 photographs of tenant farmers and workers during the Great Depression, converting the collection from an agency propaganda project to a permanent historical resource. When the records were transferred to the Library of Congress in 1944, Vanderbilt accompanied them as the first chief of the Library's Prints and Photographs Division.*

Paul took the long view of photography and shared his book collection and the archives with me. I furthered my education with him, and he hired me often as a consultant to The State Historical Society of Wisconsin to view and catalogue masses of images as well as help him compose an exhibit when he was under sharp deadlines. He was a tall, elderly, soft-spoken man, who dwelled in deep places of the mind. When he spoke, I listened. He had white hair and soft greenish-blue eyes that reflected both spark and pain. He gave me a collection of five of his gorgeous clouds and trees images, three of which hang in my living room, the other two in my bedroom. I also own a landscape photograph of his in which I can almost see myself in as the rowed fields of Wisconsin are not all that different than the rows my dogs Rumi, Roxy and I skip over when walking on the 200 acres behind my house. I often think of Paul when I'm *in* the landscape and get drawn into the clouds and trees.

After his FSA stint, Paul gravitated more and more toward nature photography and these images made up the lion's share of what he exhibited at Sunprint Gallery. I also have the storyboard layout design he drafted when we worked out the order and composition of this exhibit. Paul took a self portrait of his face reflected in a train window with trees whizzing by in the background. He merged with trees as this caption testifies: *Are we two separate entities? Or is it always me I see in trees?* He died in 1992. I was no longer living in Madison at the time and received this news almost a year after his death as we had not stayed in touch. Paul was old and lonely by this time; I remember speculating that perhaps he had a terminal illness accompanied by unbearable pain and no one to care for him. I was sad though not totally surprised. I picked handfuls of rose petals and placed them in the wooden bread bowl he had given me. I let their perfume and color fade and, with the fading, I let him go slowly and digested the loss. I have a piece of him near me everyday. He is not forgotten.

Next to Paul's work hangs an erotic image Tom M. gave me signed *To JoAnna with Love.* The subject of Tom's photography, along the lines of the famous Helmut Newton, could be called fashion erotica. His photographic mastery resides in his use of the lower zones, grays and blacks, the use of motion, and the erotic tension it captures. He had worked for ten years as special assignment/staff photographer with the United States Olympic Team. When Tom and I met on the shores of Lake Mendota, I was 18 years old and had just transferred from Boston College. We had separately been out for a bike ride and had stopped to rest and take in the sunset on the lake shore. I had newly received the Nikon camera gift from my brother and was hoping to learn to use it. Tom walked over, introduced himself, and we had our first conversation. Ironically, or as fate would have it, he was at the time a photography major studying with George Gambsky, the one person photography department at the University of Wisconsin, Madison. George was a protégé and graduate student of Minor White, both of whom were sticklers for rigor and immaculate control of the camera and then, only later, the darkroom. When I expressed my interest to study photography to Tom, he said he would see if he could help get me into Gambsky's entry level class, which was a feat as there was a long waiting list. We exchanged contact information and, ultimately, after an hour long interview with George in which he tested my grit, plus with Tom's help, I got in. I stored this as another angelic coincidence, or fate, or karma or something.

I worked for photographic mastery like never before: hours with my camera practicing the Zone System made famous by Ansel Adams and Minor White. This practice entailed contact sheets of images with only slight, half an F-stop changes, incremental and pain-staking. Then we had to do another series of hundreds of contact sheets using and mastering depth of field, motion, light and shadow. Diagonals running this way meant one thing and juxtaposed stillness and motion conveyed something else. And, we all struggled with Gambsky's famous question, "Where are you in the image? Who are you?" These are the same ironically spiritual questions I continually ask myself. Only when he was satisfied with camera mastery could we retreat into the darkroom: no fudging images with the wizardry of darkroom techniques. We had to get it right with the camera and hone our ability to control light and motion by fully marrying artistic vision with mechanical know-how. George was Minor White's student, tip to stern. He was influenced, as was White, by the world of Gurdjieff, who was an early 20th-century philosopher, spiritual teacher, Russian mystic, and composer of Armenian and Greek descent. Here it is again, that mystical thing that keeps following me around and tracking me down. The art, the energy, the mysticism converging in a physical manifestation: this time a photograph.

Tom M. ran, did yoga and introduced me to Roger, his friend and guru who, in retrospect, was my first teacher on my yogic path. I had just begun my foray into vegetarianism and our runs and yoga classes together reinforced and further informed this choice – again, great timing. Additionally, Tom and I shared the darkroom, photo outings, books and essays through which my knowledge increased by the days. He and I went to those work parties at Mary Allen's place together. We got to work side-by-side stacking wood and picking apples, an unusual event outside of the darkroom. Even the way he pet Mary's dog made me covet his touch, but we were not lovers during those early years. The first time Tom and I slept together, many years after we met, he photographed me again – it felt like the first time. The camera opened us into Minor White's "rare lyrical state of love." *Some day your camera may open to that rare lyrical state of love, translated into words as the 'splinter of divinity' in yourself, as it recognizes the same splinter in another.*

I had just returned from Europe for the one and only time, four years into my seven year stay, because my twin, Joe, had been in a serious motorcycle accident and was hospitalized, in traction and in the midst of nine bone grafting operations. This accident crushed the leg that was damaged when he had been bitten and dragged by a St. Bernard dog and stitched together by a surgeon when he was 14 years old or so. The seriousness of the accident called me back to Pittsburgh. I had left a storage unit of things behind in Madison thinking I'd be back in a few months and resume school. That didn't happen. Now back in the U.S., I wanted to make it to Madison and clear out my stuff. I called Tom after four years of silence. He picked me up at the airport, and helped me weed through the piles of things I had to winnow down to nearly nothing. We spent four or five days together sorting and making love and sorting and making love. We didn't see each other again until I permanently moved back to the States in 1976 settling in Madison again, returning to the university to finish my degree and add to it.

Our relationship spanned decades and its echo reverberates bone deep because of our stunning erotic bond and our resonance in the arts/photography. We were a pair. Tom stirred and deepened my desire for erotic love, and I deepened his, I hope. He took me there and held me close as we enjoyed the rippling, spiraling effects of simultaneous orgasm. The communion of mind and body we shared drew on something as yet undiscovered in me. He was a few years older than I, far more experienced and seductive. Individually, we each possessed a capacity for intellectual and physical union, and we took flight together. One night after hours of standing side-by-side in the darkroom, we ate dinner, had brownies with coffee for dessert and then drank Chartreuse, his favorite liquor. He stayed at my place. I was living in a big yellow house not unlike the one in a childhood repetitive dream.

I remember us sitting on the floor and Tom following the seam of my jeans with his finger during an extended hour-long conversation. He was never in a hurry. We held the large coffee table book *Tantra Asana* on our laps, a gift from my art dealer/psychiatrist friend, Pam. While looking at the erotic imagery, we absorbed Hindu script, sipped a heady liquor, digested dinner, and discussed Minor White's photo imagery as it related to mantra. We were referring to White's remarkable treatise *Mirrors Messages Manifestations*. Minor White was our teacher too. We examined his unique photographic approach: *bent light koans* and *inner landscapes*. Minor White was a heavy weight, abstract image maker who embarked on a more inward path than his friends Edward Weston and Alfred Stieglitz. He founded and became editor of Aperture magazine, which Tom and I studied and read together. We moved onto to White's premise: *the subject is always Me*. In his abstract images, White was aware of the camera as a tool to mirror the self if you practice and gain mastery, *Maybe later, much later, camera may be a means of Self growth*. We were on an intellectual bender of such a magnitude that I nearly remember it word-for-word now, some 40 years later. The camera as both *channel and barrier*, always glass between you and the world. We lived the paradox. He photographed me many times, not that night, but often. He played with me, sweetly, and set the bar high. Most importantly, he enjoyed having a travel companion who was his match in verve and intellect. He took as much pleasure as I did in the state of ecstasy we created together, tenderly and slowly. Tom and I never lived together and never declared ourselves a couple. There was no moment of commitment and then a tragic moment of breaking up. It faded in and out over many years, and I bear no scars of loss or endings in association with Tom. He remains with me, and I still smile at the thought of him. He left his mark.

Tantra Asana

We drank Chartreuse
bright as lightning bugs.
He touched the back of my neck
slowly and without hunger.

Words ceased
touch lingered
beside my breast,
behind my ear
in the crook of my elbow –
A web of erotic threads
ensnaring me in
my rising desire for him and
flamed by his quiet languor.

We rolled and he rolled
Onto me and into me
Then me, onto him where,
reflected in his eyes,
dark as tidal pools,
me and the luminous clouds overhead
solarized, floating, quivering
became a photograph of us.

I still value a man who can take me out beyond myself and into an expanded state of unity where the whole is far greater than the sum of its parts. It is rare. For this to happen, a soft safety is a given, and then the merging is fully absorbing and lyrical. The word absorption comes to mind again, a state in which I am fully present yet taken up and into all dimensions of my being. The experience bears resemblance to the meditative state as it combines the abstract with an ethereal clarity. In Pantanjali's "Yoga Sutras" he calls this state *non distinguished cognitive absorption.*

During one of my many inquiries to explain my personal mystical phenomena, I learned about micro and macro cosmic orbits and connecting and tapping into a lover's sphere. As my drive or eros is strong, I sometimes sought sexual pleasure in the absence of love or communion. For me, sexual attraction ranges from the purely physical to the nearly divine/sublime. With Tom, it was the latter. Tom and I met on bicycles, another reoccurring theme hatched in a childhood dream. I met Tom R. years later on our matching Pinarellos – wild, really, when I think of this and how it too relates to a repetitive childhood dream, which went like this: It began when I would get up out of bed in the dark on a full moon night. Quietly, I edged my bike out of the garage and began to ride with speed toward some deeply known destination. My long straight hair rose and fell on my shoulders and back. My face tilted up toward the full moon. I rode happily through the woods on a smooth mud path as the bike and I were one. At a certain point, the path went downhill steeply then rose steeply up, so I hunkered down and got serious about the effort. Head down and standing on the pedals, I pushed until I came to a point where I was nearly at a standstill and feeling unable to make it up the last five brutally steep feet. I looked up at that moment, and there I saw a Y-shaped tree in front of a romantic, yellow house lit softly and ivy-covered in places. A man stood in that Y with a hat on. Just as I gave up, and not one second before, he reached out and put his strong arm around my waist and swept me into the house. I was not afraid.

It's uncanny how even in the dream I somehow expected it, welcomed it and surrendered to the magical timing and embrace. My unknown destination became clear: it was to a man bringing me into the house (self), which I was riding toward with subconscious fury. Funny how when I had my repetitive dreams, I only vaguely remembered the outcome, so each time it occurred it was only somewhat familiar yet ecstatically vivid with eros, moonlight and sweet surrender. When I met both Tom M. and Tom R., this dream came forward as they each arrived on bicycles, brought me home in significant ways, there were yellow houses and the road home was unmistakably tantric.

Many years later, I began a serious foray into a decade-long study of esoteric yoga beginning officially in 2001 when I attended a yoga conference in Boston; I had been introduced to yoga as a college student and had dabbled ever since. I was particularly interested in a workshop on the *bandas* taught by Rod Stryker. My local teacher, Emily Garrett, brought the event to my attention, as I had asked her many questions about when to hold and when to release the three inner locks or *bandas* while practicing yoga. She too wanted to learn more, so we traveled to Boston together to attend this event. Both Emily and Rod became and remain my most cherished teachers. Rod Stryker is the founder of ParaYoga and is a renowned tantric teacher in the Hindu tradition. During this era of deep practice and study, I read my way through dozens of books, learned breath techniques, sat in meditation countless hours, and practiced daily *asanas*, the physical practice. I attended as many classes and workshops as I could afford and eventually completed my teacher training certificate in Vermont with Emily. Rod lives and teaches in Colorado and, once again, my brother Ed was supportive of my development by letting me stay at his place in Aspen and borrow his car to attend a few of Rod's five-day intensives.

The work with *bandas* interested me greatly as they are the key to containing and conserving energy within the body and learning how not to leak energy unintentionally, which is at the core of tantric yoga. This work corresponded well with a behavioral interest in boundaries and conservation of energy in order to focus on my areas of interest. The evaluation and comparison of Buddhist and Hindu traditions led me definitively toward Hinduism, a practice encouraging prosperity, abundance, and active engagement in transformation of self and society. Reevaluating habits and developing discipline has affected all areas of my life. Being present while trying to develop a future vision of self is challenging for me, as I have always had a weak sense of future. My teacher, Rod, emphasized the importance of this sense of future as a form of liberation. More of less, he says, a person will be chronically determined by their past if they cannot intentionally articulate and move toward a future self.

Hinduism appealed to me, as Buddhism tends toward a more passive acceptance of the "what is," too reminiscent of the punishing, self-depriving sadness and resignation inherent in the idea of original sin that I so resent in Catholicism. In the last four years, I have had the luxury to take two trips to Nepal to visit my daughter, Amanda. Traveling in and around Nepal with my expert-guide daughter, who has lived there for five-plus years, served to further deepen my understanding and awe of eastern spiritual traditions. The numerous sacred sights lent authenticity to my studies. Currently, I use my teacher training only once a year to lead a week long course in the White Mountains. Otherwise, the grace and depth of study and practice is reserved to enhance my personal practice, daily life and my stance in the world in countless ways.

The western attraction to eastern traditions is epidemic today and, it is not lost on me to see how, westerners raised on individualism, myself included, indulge in certain distortions. However, with a great teacher/guru, study and dedication, even the illusion of being an individual is challenged and profound transformation can occur. To be steeped in the tradition of yoga remains a privilege that is both private and revelatory for me. As a featured student at Laughing River Yoga (LRY), where I completed my teacher training, I wrote the following about the importance of yoga in my life: *I practice yoga to create more freedom in my mind and body and to open energetic channels in support of my growth and health. Also, as I am in a healing profession, I want and need to nourish myself so that I can bring a high level of clarity and energy to my work without depletion. Yoga addresses the physical, mental and spiritual as an all encompassing practice – I love to study it, move in it, and sit with it.*

I completed my teacher training in 2011, not in an effort to become a teacher, but rather to deepen my practice and be more fully immersed. After attending a hiking week at Cold River Camp in the White Mountains last summer, however, I was asked to lead a yoga week there each summer. This and the LRY invitation to feature me is so meaningful because it signals that the yogini in me is becoming more visible! No doubt, the mothering and professional aspects of my life are lived "out loud," yet daily – quietly, I live and breathe as a writer and a spiritual being – perhaps this is coming more and more to the surface with age?

The interior is a monumental source of infinite inspiration and exploration for me. As mentioned, I go underground to preserve my soul and my sanity: the result is a deep interiority. There, my reflections, fears, dreams and ideas became candescent, as if lit by candlelight. When I read Anais Nin's diaries as a young woman, I was struck by her acknowledgment of the importance of voice and process. I saw a friend in her as she recognized a quality in herself she called "an immediate awareness," and she too struggled to reconcile disparate elements in her character. Her diaries took me through her interior labyrinth in an effort to make sense of life through the filter of her sensibilities. ...*All matter must be fused this way through the lens of my vice or the rust of living would slow down my rhythm to a sob.* Her rendition of her life in these multiple volumes were as seductive as they were freeing for me. Here was a woman's interior laid bare with all the self-doubt and beauty that composed her song of life. She expressed the erotic, the tender, the esoteric. It impressed me that she satisfied her needs without much guilt. She had a therapist, Otto Rank, who became her lover; she also had a lover in the author, Henry Miller and, simultaneously a husband, Rupert Pole. I enjoyed vicariously the combination of these men as what one had the other did not. No doubt, I too have struggled to find a comfortable home for the tensions I experience in relation to wanting freedom and committed love. Men disappoint me if they don't demonstrate a nuanced understanding for disparate elements in themselves and in me. For my 40th birthday, my girls bought me a stuffed animal dog with a sweet brown spot over one eye – I named him HenryO after Anais' combined male lovers. Her husband did not impress me. I bought two matching stuffed-animal puppies for them. I travel and sleep with HenryO to this day, which reminds me of the reach for perfection in my daughters and in men.

Through the years, many memoirs, diaries, letters, biographies and autobiographies have fleshed out my interest in the stories of individual lives. The concept of "voice" is developed to my satisfaction only in this medium. When I hear National Public Radio's *Story Core* or the *Moth Radio Hour* or maybe, most especially, listen to the hundreds of adolescent students who have revealed their dreams and doubts in my office, I am stirred. Sometimes I am stirred into a reflection on my own life or, maybe, to a period in history, or I move into the reality of a child or, consistent with a sense of gender fluidity, a male narrator. The wonder and mystery packed into the human condition comes alive for me through these stories.

Self-love, the dissolving of gender, and the autoerotic as part of love and sexuality are topics Nin explores as part of her journey to self-discovery. Though considered sinful or taboo by some, no true autonomy is achieved without knowing how to love and comfort oneself at some level. Many children, like myself, were not held and cuddled enough. Well into adulthood and aging, there are periods of time when men and women are not in sustained relationships or have asexual relationships. I am one of those adults. Thumb sucking and masturbation are on the same self-comfort spectrum and appear to be natural and healthy parts of life to me. Many studies and physicians recognize the health benefits of intimacy and sexual stimulation including masturbation. I believe self-love includes all of this.

As a woman with no gender identity questions, I possess a certain androgyny without, of course, having known that word as a child. With a male/female body type and gender neutral mental and emotional characteristics, I don't fit into the ultra-feminine category. The sexual freedom and a somewhat cutting intellect gives me a cool courage and increases my loneliness. Androgyny, like autoeroticism, speaks to the introverted and brings with it a sexually mysterious and self-contained vibe. No doubt, I see these qualities as contributing both to my successes and my failures in relationships with men.

The subject of the interior of a human being fascinates me. As a child, I spent many hours, days, years alone in my interior. I also spent time wondering what other people thought about when they weren't talking. I came to feel that I couldn't really know someone unless I knew where their mind went in their "down time." My questions were often directed along some version of "a penny for your thoughts." As an adult, I continue to value the essence of the interior, mine and others. When someone lacks transparency, is taciturn and reluctant to share what's going on beneath the surface, I grow both curious and suspicious. Are they dreamy and diffuse with no urgency to verbalize, or are they hiding? Do they have nothing to say? Are they shy, unconscious, afraid, private? Can they get underneath the surface static, go down-under, mine the gold? I think authentic people are individuals who develop and use inner processes to create meaning. Having an inner life and sharing it are vastly different inclinations. But I am certain that anyone living a superficial, unexamined life is unappealing to me.

Back to the interior, what is it about people who do and who do not have a rich inner life? Is there a clear divide here between the haves and the have nots? It appears to be so to me; I have experienced a certain jealous or fear response to the deep wellspring of my interior. Always eager to learn, I began to reflect again on my urge to photograph and write poetry and the inherent relationship of the two art forms as driven by the archival instinct. A delicate discernment and fierce economy typifies both poetry and image making. Both art forms require an almost voyeuristic approach to people and experience. A witnessing, watchful eye is part of 'living autobiographically," a term coined by Paul John Eakin. Writing and photography pull on reality, yet those real people and experiences are lived and transformed all at once. It is not as cold-hearted as it may appear. It is the act of constructing a narrative of your life, making sense by looking back and, yes, of remaining distant. For me, it is a habit and a necessity and maybe it is a byproduct of having had a certain form of estrangement in my upbringing. I came by *living autobiographically* honestly and early. I felt *in* but not *of* my family, Catholicism, even girlhood, womanhood and the world somehow. My disposition and intensity took me aloft. Aloft does not imply superiority but rather hovering above and aloof in those moments when I could not participate or relate.

I have known a few cryptic men. The first sustained relationship I had after my divorce was with a very secretive person, Tom R. Though he was connecting, sexy and affectionate to me, beneath was a vast wilderness I never came to know. He worked in D.C. in some capacity for the Secret Service. He had black hair and warm, clear blue eyes. We met on the Pan Mass Challenge bike ride, which I attended for the first time with a biking friend from Vermont. Biking has been my sport of choice throughout my adulthood, maybe it started with my red Schwinn and my childhood repetitive dream? For my 40th birthday I didn't want the proposed Cartier watch but instead asked for a Pinarello bicycle. We were on sabbatical living in France for a year, and we traveled to Italy where I was fitted by Mr. Pinerello himself. Each tube length of the bike was made to my measurements, the components exquisite and the color a vibrant, classic Pinerello blue. I was at the Sturbridge start of the Pan Mass Challenge and up at 5:00 a.m. getting ready for the 170-plus mile, two-day ride to Provincetown. I was heading toward the start and looking for the pumping station to get my tires up to par. "Nice bike," I heard someone say and looked in that direction to see this handsome man in front of his bike – the identical blue Pinarello twin to mine. It was a crystal ball kind of moment. He pumped my tires and later caught up with me or, I should say, dropped back to find me at about 20 miles into that morning's ride. There was chemistry and twin bikes and my dream.

Earlier that summer, my husband, Willy, the girls and I had spent a month in Deauville at his family's annual *rendevous* in France. His father, Dede, loved to gamble and the casino at Deauville together with the ocean, the food, and the grand hotel made for a great vacation spot. We had been there many times and had even brought our dog, Max, with us who ate in sterling silver bowls placed by white gloved waiters under the table. Very *la-di-da*. I can still taste the Turbot and *haricot vert*, and see the mounds of berries with *crème fraîche* for dessert. In any event, the summer of 1992 was particularly fatal to our marriage, which had been lurching along for years in the draining energy of infidelity.

Willy was to turn 40 the following November and at one of the many hour-long lunches, in the midst of toasting this and that, his Uncle Max asked Willy what he planned to do to celebrate his 40th birthday. With that, Willy took the floor and without a pause listed the several grand trips he intended to take that year, none of which included me. He described the Chamonix-Zermatt Haute Route with his cousin, Paul and two other exotic, athletic adventures one with Max and the other, with whom? China, Romania, Rio? I forget. I was infuriated and humiliated in front of the 15 or so family members at the table. Only I explicitly knew of the other women in this port and that city though in the French/Latin culture of his family, probably every male at the table was living some version of stay-at-home wife and sleeping-around husband. But I didn't sign on for that life, and my naiveté was finally catching up with me. Here again I think of Henry James' spirited character, Isabel Archer, who gets pulled into a deceit unimaginable to her. Like her, I am committed to my independence and have the existential willingness to bear the consequences of my choices with integrity. Like Isabel, I have crossed over cultural lines and have been surprised by motives I didn't fully understand. It became clear to me that summer that I could no longer travel the distance. So often over the years when speaking with my father on the phone, he would ask to speak to Willy. He's in China, Thailand, France, Mexico…."Again," my Dad would say, "You live a goddamn lonely life."

CHARLOTTE TO BEIJING

My husband, so many weeks away
is somewhere in the pointed mountains
and rice fields of a Chinese landscape.
His head an orb on slanted shoulders
as he boyscouts on a bamboo raft
along the Yellow River
or in the traffic of the Yangtze.
He might stop to admire a painted stone
before returning to the darkness
of his room, to sleep on a narrow bunk
heavy with woolen, grey blankets.

As for me, my bed is laid light
with feathers and Egyptian cottons
to offset the other heaviness.
Domestic things are the same,
days tick by much as they have
these most recent years in Vermont
where a spin of need calls out to me
from the children and the kitchen,
the animals and the wood stove.

The lake outside the study window
more pewter than ever, swallows
the purples and hazy peaches
of the sky at dusk and dawn.
The gray waters surge and, when
I look way out, I get somehow drifting
on the swell of currents out there
in the midst of all that gray.

My head is low, my back is curled in on itself
like the wooden spine of my paint-chipped canoe.
My vessel can float for hours and then
suddenly stick in the swirling water-grasses
where even eels lose themselves, willingly,
at the midday of their slippery swim.

Struggling already with defeat and despair, I was doing my best to carry on in this sham of a relationship. So at this lunch, I felt the hair rise up the back of my neck and my pulse accelerate. It was the moment that the guillotine blade descended on the already weak cord of connection holding me in the marriage. I had thought of leaving many times as the marriage dynamic was growing ever more toxic. In the previous year, he had had some risky sex in Thailand, yet he had been sleeping with me nonetheless. At this juncture, I moved from humiliation to realization that my husband was putting my life at risk both emotionally and physically: I did not want STDs or AIDS.

On that afternoon, in gorgeous Normandy, I worked hard at composure and couldn't wait to throw off my fancy clothes and walk into my decision on the beach. I was pregnant with that decision to divorce and gave birth to it that afternoon. Insulted to be relegated to home and child care while my husband traveled throughout the upcoming year flagrantly sleeping with this one and that one was not going to come to an end. My father-in-law, Dede, and I were very close and before I left on my four-hour walk alone with my journal, I confided in him that I was grievously offended and half out the door of the marriage. I did walk and write my way into a decision that day. I vowed to myself that I would begin divorce proceedings and be on my way out before my 45th birthday that December, and I did.

Just as I walked into that decision on Normandy beach, I rode my bike out of the marriage at the Pan Mass Challenge that August. Willy and the girls stayed in Europe with his family. I returned home and set out on the planned bike ride with a neighbor friend, who introduced me to the idea. When I heard "nice bike" and saw this man with the exact bike as mine, the puzzle pieces of fate slid closer together. I was in tip-top shape in those days, and Tom was too. We rode both days together, side-by-side, sometimes silent, sometimes in conversation, always in harmony. It was a magical weekend: perfect weather and strong chemistry, expert riding and the nearly fictional image of these two magnificent bicycles in flight or leaning against a tree together during the food breaks. My childhood dream, my marital strife, my prayers to the universe for a way out and forward all converged.

It is hard to gloss over my 13 years of marriage and its end. There were many things about my life with Willy, home ownership, gardening and travel that made me a better person and offered me opportunities that I had not had before. He is smart and courted me royally. My passion for food and cooking took on new heights during the course of our marriage. Our first extended date was traveling to Seattle for a week to hear Wagner's Ring in its entirety in the evenings and hike bits and pieces of Mt. Rainier during the days. His family didn't like me at first but eventually took me in and, though I need a complete separate memoir to delve into the beauty of motherhood, without Willy I wouldn't have Amanda and Deva and that is an untenable prospect. But I suffered and was embarrassed by Willy's infidelities over the course of many years and was tired of his assumptions that it was alright to leave me at home with the domestic responsibilities while he lived a life of complete freedom.

After Dinner

Red wine made me sultry
we fought
bruising us again
already tense as lightning.

I seek silence in the summer night
sit on the raw boards of our porch
look south into darkness
collect myself, or try

stars pierce the sky
shine down on misty fields
and mingle with lightening bugs.

There are inevitable distortions in this kind of festering, in looking for solutions, a way out, I found one in Tom. So after the breakup of my marriage, I had five blissful years with him. He visited often, always with a present for me and my daughters. He helped me with three miserable moves from house to house to house and listened to the drama and trauma of my divorce proceedings and stalls. During those years, the girls and I traveled to Arlington, Virginia, where Tom lived for a spectacular 4th of July picnic under the Washington Monument. He attended my father's funeral with us. Our trip to Ottawa for ice skating on the canals one January was unforgettable as were the camping trips he and I took to Lobster Lake in Maine. There, we rowed our canoe for hours, lingered on mini islands, made love and slept under the stars. Once a moose trampled close to our tent, and he held me as I shook all over. Laughing and nuzzling the back of my neck, he put me back to sleep. We had a rare love and he was a deep lover; I felt whole and loved.

LACE

There are those days
when dreams accompany me
out of bed
down the stairs
where I still wear love
under my nightgown
next to my skin.

Laughing, my eyes dance the kitchen
taking in counter crumbs
with no grudge toward
the dog, the man or the children.

The day unfolds, stick by stick
making squash soup, then apple pie
and, at the end of those days
we've made lace.

He had been a Division 1 hockey player for University of Massachusetts, Amherst and the class president. He loved to skate. Born in Lowell into relative poverty, he managed with sports and merit scholarships to graduate and get recruited by the Navy and, I think, do high risk missions of some sort or another. Maybe he was a Navy Seal? He had the sharp physical and mental acumen for it. The secretiveness started there and ended with my learning that he had a past relationship with someone named Jane, whom he returned to ultimately or maybe had never really left?

I was in love with this man, so the pain and heartache that accompanied this outcome cannot be relived without the memory of laying prostrate on the floor on my belly and sobbing for days. It was around the Christmas holidays and the girls were thankfully away with their father in Mexico where they annually celebrate New Year's Eve. Tom was supposed to visit, and I had presents for him wrapped under the tree. He kept making excuses, said he was overseas on some mission or another and couldn't make it. He kept stringing me on, maybe in a few days…. On January 2, 2000, I was cross country skiing at Trapp's Family Lodge in Stowe with my since deceased friend, Brad. We had paused at the cabin, and I sat on the porch drinking hot chocolate when it came to me like a bell ringing: he is with Jane. This was another one of those mystical moments as I was in nature, stillness set in and opened me to this revelation. Years earlier, we had had a talk about his relationship history and he told me about her with a certain tenderness. At the time, it never occurred to me that she was a threat of any kind. I am not sure she was then nor how or when Tom hooked up with her again, but he did and didn't have the courage to tell me.

Another collision of values and shake-up had come earlier when Tom wanted me to move to the D.C. area with the girls. He couldn't imagine himself quitting his job and moving to live with me and the girls in a town where my irate ex-husband lived.

I was renting and moving from expensive house to expensive house in Charlotte in order to keep Amanda and Deva in their school and home. Getting divorced was a full time job while I was applying to masters' programs in the area. My lawyer and I fully intended to get my education paid for and shorten alimony. Though not the most financially beneficial plan, dependency on a man who hated me and wished me to "end up on a street corner with a tin cup" was not an option for me. As a sidebar, my lawyer suspected that Willy would pick up and move back to Mexico, which would make collecting alimony from a man who fought giving me any support hard to track down.

I was caught in a crossfire of values and desires. As a woman, I was deeply in love with Tom and saw myself possibly marrying him and, as a mother, my prime concern was to be with my daughters and avoid any further disruption to their lives. I entered the divorce plea seeking full custody. Willy retaliated by making it clear he would fight me to death for full custody. With his deep pockets and escape hatch to Mexico, I was afraid I could have lost that battle and, more tragically, the children. Joint custody can only be negotiated if both parents agree. If one parent goes for full custody and the other wants custody for whatever reason, a court battle ensues. As a full-time mother with part-time work in a marriage where Willy's travel, infidelities and absences were easily provable, I should have won. But there were other things at play here for me. First, my lawyer and I were frankly surprised that Willy wanted custody. Though we questioned his motives and his ability to sustain it, we had to regroup and respond. It was time to make some tricky calculations.

My daily meditation practice held another kind of sway over me. I went to the mat and the cushion and sat with this question: Who am I to deny my children a relationship with their father? Regardless of his flagrant shenanigans, Willy is a family man. As a Jew, and a man raised in Latin America by committed parents, he, like me, has well-defined values regarding parenthood. These values, besides the love we felt for each other, are some of what I saw in Willy and, likewise, what he saw in me. In his own way, he loved me and his daughters; I don't question that. However, the other ethnic and character-based factors that informed his manhood brought him out of that family role on a regular basis. It was clear to me how that made him a far worse husband than a father. I went with the wisdom of the meditative insights and, while I knew it would be a torturous journey for me to be in any form of cooperative relationship with Willy, which proved nearly impossible many times, and I knew my children would suffer from his aggressive narcissism and our tensions often, and they have, I did not want the responsibility of his absence from their lives. In 1996, I was officially divorced with joint custody after a miserable, expensive and painful divorce battle.

Marriage confounds me! My parents were married for 63 years, did not model good relationship skills and spread way too much misery on their children along the way. I had married for life, I thought. I was 32 years old, experienced, educated and gainfully employed in a thriving, self-conceived photography and food business, Sunprint Gallery. My independence had been tested and proven, and now I wanted children. A man with an education, European and multi-ethnic, athletic, interested in food and the arts, and in love with me seemed right.

During the two and a half years between mutual decision, proposal, and the wedding, much transpired that brought its share of scars and doubts. First, Willy's mother, Lucette, was not a big fan of me as a match for her son. I was five years older and not Jewish. She protested and had considerable sway over Willy. On the other hand, his father met me, and we instantly adored each other. He put up little resistance to our marriage plans. Next, I got pregnant. I had been worried about being infertile as a result of my illegal abortion with the ensuing infection and scar tissue and only used birth control, the unwieldy diaphragm, when I thought I could be ovulating. Willy was cavalier about it and found the prospect/risk of me being pregnant as sexy and with a *so-what-we're getting-married* dismissal. Well, I was thrilled to be pregnant of course, but his mother, probably both parents at this point, were not in favor of this at all! They were so adamant about this being a bad start and probably suspicious that I had "tricked" Willy into marriage that it caused a storm in Willy. He wanted me to have an abortion now. I was incensed by his turncoat attitude and his wandering over to the side of his parents. He threatened not to marry me and to have nothing to do with me or the child if I went ahead with the pregnancy. More red flags that I chose to ignore.

The old message of being "too much," which was the kernel message I received from my mother in her racist and punishing fashion, haunted my relationships with men too. If my mother witnessed any boundless vitality, of which I had plenty, she would compare me to Aunt Rosie who, in her disparaging view of all of our Lebanese relatives, laughed too much, and danced with too much "oomph." Aunt Rosie, who married her first cousin, my Uncle Bill, sang in nightclubs wearing deep red lipstick. She flirted and fought with her husband and wore sexy dresses. She was alive, sexual, vibrant, Lebanese and was held up by my mother as an example of all that was evil and undesirable. Undoubtedly, this early messaging helped set the stage for my willingness to repress my very essence and collapse under pressure.

This pre-marriage situation along with many others to follow pitted me squarely against myself in unfortunate ways. It also put me in an adversarial battle-of-the-wills relationship with Willy where I caught a fatal glimpse of his primary allegiance to his mother and his ability to threaten and manipulate me. These dynamics started early and lasted throughout my marriage; on some level, being complicit against myself would haunt me, our marriage and ultimately lead to our divorce. I was sleeping with the enemy. I got an abortion and went forward with the marriage only to be unable to conceive a child. The medium was right, I would have to work for it. Luckily, the patency of my fallopian tubes were ultimately restored through a successful laser tubalplasty by a maverick surgeon from Cornell Medical Center. Lasar surgery on fallopian tubes to minimize scarring was a brand new procedure at the time. My friend Pam, then studying to become a doctor herself, made this connection for me. As she had been a part of my loss of fertility, she was part of my regaining it too. Good karma for her and me, and I was one of the lucky ones!

Childbirth and motherhood was and remains pure wonder! Coming from an inadequate mother, I was keen not to make any of the same mistakes, which may actually have lead to a mistake of overcompensation. Nonetheless, this was not a heady decision but rather grew out of innate heart healthiness and a robust animal / maternal instinct. Before becoming a mother at 36 years old, I had done extensive soul searching, self discovery and healing. I had already realized myself professionally, enjoyed years of formal education, reading, meditating, cooking and working. I had "suffered in bed" to regain my fertility and consciously readied myself for motherhood, an easy undertaking. Pregnancy was challenging but birth and motherhood felt like second nature to me. I gave myself over to it with joy accompanied by the lessons of having a cold and distant mother. I was lucky to have a husband who provided well for us, so I did not have to work for a living during these years, though I did continue to work part-time. Amanda was born in 1985 and Deva in 1987, only 29 months apart. Once Deva was born, I was fortunate to be able to modify my work schedule and my position at *Harrowsmith Magazine* and still keep my job. Before that, when I was pregnant with Amanda, I had recently help design the certificate program in graphic arts and photography at the University of Vermont's Church Street Center. I was teaching photography in that program up to the delivery of Amanda. It was a humbling experience as my nausea was constant but unpredictable. Often I would be in the middle of instruction in front of a room of 15-25 students and all of a sudden I would begin to throw up in my hand – I had no notice it was coming on. It was kind of funny, so we all laughed nervously.

Though pregnancy was not my finest hour, as I had morning sickness from conception to the delivery table, I was keen enough to know it was the road to a deeply desired outcome. As such, the idea of pregnancy held me utterly captive. As I was 36 years old when I was pregnant with Amanda, we had all the usual high-risk testing done including amniocentesis during which Willy fainted to the ground when they inserted the long needle into my abdomen. We learned we were having a girl and chose her name. We were living in a charming old house in Charlotte, Vermont at the time, and I threw myself into nesting and sewing when I wasn't working or recovering from a nasty vomiting bout over the toilet. Milkshakes settled my stomach and inched me toward a 50 lb. weight gain – I had never had such an abundant body and enjoyed feeling opulent along with the sensations of our baby moving and kicking inside of me. Both pregnancies and births followed a similar trajectory; I had midwife deliveries in a hospital supported by backup. Each delivery had the usual hours of painful contractions, but the actual moments of birth were unexaggeratedly orgasmic. Immediately, my mother-bear instinct to covet and protect, my desire to have my babies go from *in* my belly to *on* my belly, to breast feed on demand, and never let them out of my sight was engaged. The bittersweet part was that it cast a gun-metal-gray shadow on an already dark stain of my beginnings. It made what my mother had done, left me in the hospital for 28 days in the unmotherly arms of nuns with no apparent animal urge to hold me, give me her breast and marvel over my newborn perfection seem like an incredulous travesty. Willy's parent's traveled to Vermont for both births and generously helped us with food preparations and baby love. I did not want my mother any where near me or my babies at this time in my life.

Afterwards, I took the steps three at a time when they awoke from their naps. I lay in the hammock and nursed for hours. I wore a green and white checkered square dancing skirt and an oversized white shirt. I was so full bodied that this generous skirt was one of the few items of clothing that didn't confine and hurt. My breasts went from minimal hills to an E-cup, blue-veined and flowing with milk. I loved this luscious feeling and indulged myself and them in the yumminess of it all. I gladly retreated from my work place into a home office, from Food Editor to Cookbook Editor for *Harrowsmith Magazine*, allowing me to relish in the dreamy pleasure of how my babies smelled and looked. It was a languid time not in any way typical of other phases and stages of my life. I was grateful for the invitation to lean in and sleep cuddled up, to dally with the hose on a hot summer's day, and cherish the miracle and gift of knowing and caring for two beautiful, healthy little girls.

The blissful intimacy, the heart-expanding love, the beauty of both daughters' wholeness moved me deeply. I felt like a figure in the gorgeous Chagall murals in Lincoln Center in New York City, where figures float in a pool of red and indigo blue, arms outstretched overhead playing musical instruments or just reaching. I was buoyant, and my only job was to float in a sea of love, to reach toward my girls and guide them gently, this way and that, to keep them on the course they had already pre-chosen. I see my daughters as globes, a world unto themselves, complete and whole. I floated and touched them as often as I could without interfering with their soaring development. I cannot imagine life without them. I cluck like a mother hen with joy when they are near me, and roar like a beast of prey at anyone who tries to hurt them. Their beauty astonishes me. Happily, I did not fully know of or, more likely, let myself accept my husband's infidelities at this time, which would have marred these most precious years.

Mothering took a turn after the divorce as I had to go back to school and get a masters degree in order to provide, move houses until I could afford to buy one, and regroup on multiple levels. During my years of hard work, shouldering the financial and emotional responsibilities of single parenting, I mourned the loss of my creativity; I had no wiggle room to be frivolous. Motherhood came first without question, but I am well aware of how my romantic relationships and creative life got squeezed into the margins. Here I refer to what I call the "blank page creativity." Starting with nothing and attempting to pursue a new direction was too much of a reach, too impractical, I thought. I did not get the dreamed of MFA in writing, but rather an M.Ed.

No doubt some of my creative energy went toward constructing a new family identity for the girls and me. Things were radically different and extremely tense for all of us, especially the girls during this extended transitional phase. They went back and forth between two households, two computer systems, two vastly different incomes, two ways of being in the world. What was once a unified family was now split into two warring nations. The divorce proceedings went painfully slow as Willy resisted the idea and wanted to make it as difficult as possible for me to succeed. Sadly, the girls were caught in the crossfire. I wish I had handled this better, but I clearly didn't have a deep enough reserve emotionally or financially to dig deep and do well.

Just as all great civilizations use architecture to manifest national identity, I intuitively knew we had to build a new family identity. For a while, we were in temporary rentals and I was working and simultaneously finishing my master's degree in

Education. I was hanging on by the proverbial thread and just surviving! But after moving three times before buying a house, getting settled meant creating our own holidays. We got out the baking pans, my sewing machine and bag of fabric remnants at the advent of each holiday and started sewing and baking our way into a sense of home. For Valentine's Day, we sewed little overalls for our matching stuffed animals; the fabric was a flutter of red hearts, of course. These stuffed animals, HenryO included, were set up at the iconic dining room table, rescued in Austria from a farmer's scrap heap and with me ever since. We used our heart-shaped cookie cutters to make pancakes for breakfast. The table was awash with doilies and construction paper hearts. When Christmas was nearing, we made our own stockings with black and white wool remnants and fragments of lace and chiffon left over from sewing my wedding dress. I pulled out jars of buttons as ornaments. The floor and table were strewn with bits of lace, buttons and once-folded reams of fabric. We each got to choose how we wanted our stockings to look but, by using the same pattern, we matched them in size and shape to provide a sense of family unity. I did most of the sewing, but guided the girls' little hands under mine when they wanted to sew for themselves. My creativity was funneled into homemaking and mothering and to this day, each time I bring those treasured stockings or overalls out for the holidays, I smile in memory of our messy, fun-filled days of making them together.

My ex-husband kept the house on the lake as he wanted it, and I did not have the means to support it. No doubt, land on the lake on a dead end street in Charlotte is of great value, but I never loved the house; it was never home to me. By the time we bought it in the early 1990s, I was becoming aware of the deprivation in my marriage. Further, the house itself was made cheaply: door handles were ill-fitting and sliding closet doors repeatedly came off their tracks. The house was built initially by the Hill family as a summer place because the Wing's Point home with its Palladian windows and lavish lawn was sold by Patrick and Genevieve Hill to create the Wing's Point Club, where I worked for a few years soon after we first arrived. This was their summer home; they were well into their 80s and had other residences. The land and house had questionable energy, from my point of view, due to some stories told to me by their daughter, Rue. First of all, who names their child Rue? The dictionary definition of this word is "to feel sorrow over; repent, or regret bitterly." There is also a medicinal, non-culinary, semi-toxic herb called Rue or herb-of-grace, but legend has it that you need its grace to get over your sorrow. Rue was distributed by the mad Ophelia in Hamlet and planted by the gardener in Shakespeare's Richard II to mark the spot where the Queen wept when she heard news of Richard's capture. *Here did she fall a tear, here in this place / I'll set a bank of rue, sour herb of grace.*

There was a "Rue tree" planted for her in the roundabout of the driveway, she claimed, really a Linden or Black Walnut tree, I think, along with a pile of foul memories associated with the place. When her parents died, she inherited the house and couldn't wait to get rid of it. It went on the market and, upon Willy's biddings, I acted on my contact with Genevieve to plead our case. My connection with this English family is what got us the house together with a co-signature from my beloved brother, Ed. During the divorce settlement though, I didn't want the marital bed or the house. I hoped for a fresh start in a familiar town where my girls could stay in the school system and in the company of their friends. Charlotte is not an ideal town to live in as a single mom, working full time and living on meager resources, but we managed. My girls and my relationship with Tom R. brought me what little sweetness I had during those tough years.

Just as my childhood forged my character, my relationship, marriage and divorce put certain of my characteristics to the test and intensified them; I liken it to the blacksmith's fire. I recognize that I am far from an easy person. High strung and exacting, I demand as much from others as I do from myself. I am not utterly American, nor do I fit into the patriarchal version of ideal beauty or availability. I am not blonde and buxom. I am not submissive to authority. I love men, but I seriously hate the "hyper masculinity (that) sits like an elephant on steroids stinking up the living room," as Thomas Page McBee puts it in his essay "Self-Made Man." This is not the self-made man I knew my father to be, rather he was short and stocky, tender-hearted, and used his charm not to get but to give. Instead, I am curly-haired, amber-eyed, angular and muscular, athletic, fiercely independent, and principled and was married to a hyper-hoping-to-be-masculine man.

Unlike many successful wives, I have no ability to directly ask for or demand what I want from my partner. I have heard myself say many times, "If I have to ask for it, I don't want it anymore." This is not to say that I expect my friends and lovers to be mind readers, but I do expect them to be tuned in, paying attention, and listening. I value perceptive, sensitive, and thoughtful awareness above practically all else! As a lover, I believe I can and do surf the contours of my lover's heart, body and mind to be supportive and loving in a meaningful way. Still, it is fair to say that what ease I may have had prior to my failed marriage evaporated. Perhaps, the post-divorce men in my life have had my best or worst self, I am not sure. I lost some things that were, at that point, only very tentatively formed: trust and compromise. I gained the capacity to fight hard and smart for what I want and deserve. If I am disappointed and unsatisfied, my man probably quickly feels unsure about our future. Leaving my marriage took almost ten years of my life: seven just trying to muster up the courage and three to finalize the divorce from a vicious opponent. The message I convey, like it or not, is that I can leave, have done so before, and will do it again if I have to.

On the plus side, I am any man's equal.

These reinforced tendencies together with my strong relationship to my interior, my journaling habit, my strength and independence, make me a formidable partner. Still, I don't see myself as difficult as my inner landscape looks like familiar and friendly terrain to me. I have the emotional generosity, warmth and intensity of my father, and have, to learn my karmic lessons, picked emotionally unavailable men just as he picked my mother. I have never questioned my basic goodness and capacity to love. I look at my relationship life as a pendulum swinging back and forth between sexy, strong, energetic competitive men on the one side to kinder, quieter, passive and more artistic men on the other side. As I embody the above complexity, it is not always easy to find a man with this range, which is maybe why HenryO sleeps in my bed every night!

I vacillate from being in the world to retreating, from arching physicality to consuming spiritual practice, from in love to out of love. I feared becoming too rarefied and esoteric at times as my various deep interests created a wedge between myself and others. I crave depth over breadth and the deeper I go, the more people I leave behind. This is not intentional, but it is a byproduct of my character. I recognize that I do not belong easily either, so when I go to a special education conference or a gardening workshop, I look around and feel little if any connection to the room full of people. My studies and deep plunges created an eclectic toolbox that ultimately separate me from a sense of belonging to any one group. At the same time, I fight against loneliness and desperately need to be seen and loved as I am. I have often felt loved and adored by a man, but nothing has lasted a lifetime. Strong women have a hard time giving, receiving and finding committed love, I think. There is a certain aloofness that comes with independence and a strong interior life, which are threatening to many men. Maybe, too, it is because I don't want to be the center of anyone's universe, as

I don't conceive of love that way. I don't want that responsibility, and I refuse to fill emptiness in a man. I prefer two whole people coming together, even colliding, to a codependent version of love.

As mentioned earlier, I began practicing yoga and meditation in my Madison years. But I returned to study and practice in earnest again in 2000. I started by attending classes in Burlington with a woman who exuded joy and self-love. She owned a studio and offered asana classes, the physical practice of yoga, which ended in a long rest and guided meditation. It was the right thing at the right time as I was recovering from the end of my romantic relationship with Tom R. and knew that my relationship to self had to be updated and revitalized. Nothing like a swift kick in the gut to get me questioning my very existence, motives, dreams and direction. I went inside, deep into my interior, where I listened and learned. Why had I fallen in love with another man who betrayed me? Often song lyrics typify the energy behind the scenes. I resonate with Tim Hardin's *A Reason to Believe* when thinking about Tom R.: *If I listened long enough to you / I'd find a way to believe that it's all true / Knowing that you lied straight-faced while I cried / Still I looked to find a reason to believe.*

Coming from the deep center of an old wound, I could not tolerate another betrayal, another person who possessed profound cowardice in relationship to the truth. Perhaps at this time in my life, I needed to meet and love people with a cord of honesty and decency. "Not again," my psyche cried. How was it possible that I still had blindspots and naïveté? Like Isabel Archer, was I simply out of my league? Did I choose unavailable men because I was unavailable myself? Was I meant to live alone and give up on the hope of a merged and loving bond with a partner? More questions to guide my searching...

As an educational therapist, my standards of excellence are based on a mosaic of beliefs and practices gathered from my education, spiritual life, physicality and experience. A capacity for empathy, a love of freedom, and a drive to bring others to their maximum potential governs my 15 years of work with adolescents and adults in private practice. I often work for many years with a student, one-on-one, and with this luxury of time, I can create the intimacy necessary to get inside and ride the wave of their mind. Being able to see through their eyes, I experience their road blocks and their gifts. Most of my clients are diagnosed as "twice exceptional," meaning they are both gifted and have a learning disability. These students belong in the company of a fascinating group of insightful individuals as the likes of Einstein, DaVinci and Bill Gates are considered twice exceptional. I attempt to offer corrective twists and turns, model skills and cognitive processes until we find the way out of "stuckness" and into self-actualization. As a healer, I work to reflect my students' beauty and wholeness back to them with a steadiness and patience that invites them to walk in and belong – to begin to live there. This population often grapples with perfectionism, intensity, nonconformity, and loneliness. Perhaps this path mimics my journey such that I can relate. The western psychologists and neuroscientists tend to pathologize and fix. The eastern world addresses the "what is" from the perspective of neuro-diversity and with a core belief that wholeness is a birthright, which has been sometimes clouded over by disabilities, trauma, neglect or imbalances in the body and the brain. I have worked to fashion an approach that is individualized, disciplined and delicate, so the student and I can navigate the complexity with a joyful sense of exploration and hope.

Work, meditation, mothering, education, writing, biking, yoga, gardening and food have been constant steadying factors for me without which I would be a far more anxious person. After Tom, I took one of those long breaks from men. This loss leveled me flat for several years. I could not meet him halfway and bought a house on my own, not inviting him in on the ownership. It wasn't an option, as I was unwilling to ever again be in a home I could be thrown out of if a relationship failed. I had children to raise, a career to foster, and I needed time to lick my wounds. Just as the death of my nephew, Davey, took me into new realms about death and what's next, this betrayal and heartbreak centered my questioning on what was it in me that brought about my unsettling disappointments with men. I looked closely, once again, at the emotional and physical abuse patterns in my family as I had entered that territory post-divorce as well. I looked with new eyes at what I needed from men and why. I do not have a wealth of answers, but I have dwelled in the questions. *Be patient toward all that is unsolved in your heart and try to love the questions themselves, like locked rooms and like books that are now written in a very foreign tongue. Do not now seek the answers, which cannot be given you because you would not be able to live them. And the point is, to live everything. Live the questions now. Perhaps you will then gradually, without noticing it, live along some distant day into the answer. Rainer Maria Rilke*

Loving questions and bowing to mystery go hand-in-hand. Having lived with an abundance of unanswered questions about myself and the world has taught me to become friends with uncertainty and to trust the passage of time to reveal what is necessary when appropriate. Locked rooms, foreign books, and the landscape of the heart capture concrete and abstract versions of the unknown. My awareness of uncertainty started young, and I experienced how the path of learning and a dedicated spiritual practice helped cultivate patience and tolerance toward uneasiness. Remaining steady in the face of disappointment or setbacks has required a lifetime of discipline, which I am fortunate to possess and enjoy. Another version of this is identifying challenges and inching my way toward solutions. Mastery with the camera, the sewing machine, and on the balance beam has helped me tame questions into products and performances. Designing a gymnastics routine or putting together a photography exhibit requires framing the problem, naming it and then solving it. I remember in gymnastics how I wanted to rise up from horizontal to vertical several times before the dismount. For example, from the flat and horizontal Russian split, I rose up into a handstand by placing my hands between my legs and muscling up into a handstand, moving through a pike position and unfolding into a vertical shape like a needle. Shape-shifting excited me and following a conceptual solution engaged my mind along with my body. When sewing, I created other kinds of problems like how to combine crisp linen with a diaphanous silk, and I sewed my way into the solution. My first one-person exhibit of color photographs also began with a conceptual goal of exploring color and cultural qualities. The exhibit was a series of eighteen color images on cream, acid-free, 16 X 20 mount board. To introduce the exhibit, I wrote the following: *These photographs are selected from two portfolios which emerged from my travels and homesteads in Austro-Hungarian Europe and Mexico. At first, I was tempted to conclude that color is culturally determined: Europe displaying medieval, and melancholy pastels – Mexico, vital and vibrant primaries. There certainly appears to be a soft stillness in the European colors and a pregnant energy in the Mexican ones corresponding to the particulars of these cultures. That initial impression weakens over time however, and yields to an understanding of the complexity of color and the meaning of color. This complexity is the pivot of my aesthetic and brings these two portfolios together.*

The progression from duality to convergence, underscored in this statement, typifies what interests me as a thinker about nearly every realm of inquiry that intrigues me: neurology, psychology, spirituality, education, image making and word construction. It is no different to me than bringing together linen and silk, horizontal and vertical.

During the early years of single parenting, I was working and finishing my master's degree. Being in school, reading, studying and learning remains pure joy to me. If I could, I'd quit my day job and go back to school, do an intensive language immersion in Arabic or French, or attend a long-distance program and get that elusive MFA in writing I thought I'd pursue after returning from the sabbatical year in France. Participating in my education for education's sake remains a foundation and a luxury I cherish. When I attended Boston College for one year before transferring to University of Wisconsin, Madison, I sank into the Jesuit curriculum with zeal. Being part of the first class of females, BC offered only education or nursing as potential majors for women. I wanted neither but loved the way the required first-year curriculum moved up through time in a synchronized way. In every discipline, we began by studying history. English, theology, philosophy, ancient civilizations, and art – each had the same starting point, so each separate course informed all of the others. Though the state of women and the degrees offered to women in a Catholic college was shamefully archaic at the time, I benefitted from being able to learn for learning's sake. I received a true liberal arts education focused on provoking thought and discipline. Reading Martin Buber and Nietzsche in the same semester introduced me to the yank and pull of differing points of view: God is everything or God is dead. I had a single room in a brownstone in Newton, MA and a calico cat. I don't even like cats too much, but I guess a dog was out of the question. I studied fiendishly and finally realized, once and for all, that I was not a Catholic and wanted to be an English major. I wanted to try my hand at theatre, but the play being performed was *The Life of Job*. Of all the biblical stories, I hated this one most of all for it was sad, punishing, and dreary. I could see how even the exciting world of theatre was, at Boston College, tainted by religious zeal. I had lived enough of my life with such distortions and had no intentions for my foray into theatre to be twisted in this way.

Still, I continued to be intrigued by sacred texts throughout college and after. Eventually, my spiritual studies took a turn toward Buddhism and later toward Hinduism, as I began to feel that Buddhism courted passivity and suffering in ways that seemed too reminiscent of Catholicism. Though Buddhism is anchored with a redeeming quest for peace and detachment, I realized that detachment is foreign to me as a person with passionate Middle Eastern blood! I started to reevaluate my meditation practice and seek a more dynamic and interactive relationship to spirit. This held my attention and offered rich rewards. The polytheistic quality of Hinduism also appealed to me as I found I was offered a plethora of gods and goddesses and paths to enlightenment from which to choose, engaging agency and individualism in a way that I found appealing. This notion of deity choice is called *Ishta-deva*. In my examination of self, and before I could afford yoga, I had several astrological readings and began to look at my blueprint and purpose in a new light. It is worth noting that I did not seek romantic love and marriage as a means of illumination. I now gravitate to the common Kundalini mantra *Sat Nam – I am truth*. Meanwhile, my career was opening up rapidly. Though I did not get a job as an English teacher at the local high school, I did get a full-time tutoring job at Pine Ridge School, went to St. Michael's College to finish my Masters in Education degree and kept raising my daughters with deep pleasure and satisfaction.

In 1997, I found and bought a house of my own. I had moved twice and was spending three-fourths of my meager income on rent. When I was finally divorced in 1996, I could begin to look in earnest for a home I could love and afford. Charlotte is a relatively expensive town, so I struggled. Finally, I rode by the house I now own and there was a sale by owner sign outside. The phone number was one digit different than mine –

odd! I called and heard that someone was already interested, but I insisted on a tour.

Ed Stone answered the door and let me in to the sweetest cottage type house with a wood stove and cooking stove exactly like mine. Outside, it was clad in cedar shingles and was surrounded by opulent gardens. There was a small screened-in porch facing west. I stood within it and looked out at five apple trees laden with fruit. The house is 1,700-square feet with two outbuildings, one of which I thought might hold my future business though this was years down the road. Built in 1870 it had been renovated into an open floor plan and situated on only one shy acre, "grandfathered-in" as there is a five acre minimum in Charlotte. The fact that it is on a busy road and on a small plot of land kept the price affordable. I was smitten, felt I belonged, and immediately presented Ed with a $3,000 check in earnest money, which he accepted. In short, I bought this house like you buy a pair of shoes: in one afternoon with no one's input but my own. It was right and I knew it; I walked back into the land of apples once again. This is another way in which my intuition speaks to me. No regrets – I love this home. It has proven to be a fine container for both growth and happiness. I responded to a writing prompt called *Querencia* in a book called *Writing Toward Home.* Georgia Heard defines the word thus: *In Spanish, querencia describes a place where one feels* safe, *a place from which one's strength of character is drawn, a place where one feels at home.*

This quaint cottage-like house is my *querencia.* It was also an example of how something came across the conveyor belt of life, and I instantly recognized it as right. I left Pine Ridge and got hired as a tutor at The Stern Center for Language and Learning, where I solidified my training and my commitment to this work in special education. Once again, I was fortunate to have many wonderful mentors who nurtured my interest and gave me the opportunity to gain mastery in my chosen field. My career feeds me on multiple levels as it offered a cross section of disciplines in cognitive theory, neurology and psychology in the context of an intimate client-to-professional relationship. It was and is a good fit. Soon after the stint at Stern, I applied for and got the Director of Academics position back at Pine Ridge School. This was a step toward administration and furthered my experience and exposure to hundreds of students with learning disabilities and their profiles. I hired and trained teachers and modified the curriculum to meet the needs of these learners. I served on the admission's committee and read hundreds of educational evaluations over the years, which unwittingly set me up to be on my own eventually. I did research and was invited to present on morphology at an Orton-Gillingham conference in Chicago in November, 1999. Samuel T. Orton a neuropsychiatrist and Anna Gillingham, a gifted educator and psychologist, together identified the patterns in the dyslexic thinker and developed a one-on-one multi-sensory approach to student instruction known as the Orton-Gillingham approach.

I arrived in Chicago on November 2nd in time for the onset of conference and my presentation on morphology the next day. I unpacked my things and went downstairs in the hotel for a bite to eat and a glass of wine. At 9:00 p.m., I returned to my room and the phone rang. It was my sister, Jane, calling to let me know that Dad had just died in the hospital. Hearing that news when alone in an unfamiliar city made the shock of a my father's death feel even more surreal and alienating. I put on my coat and set out onto the streets at night. The hotel was in a safe part of the city. I walked and walked and shook with sobs, wrapping my coat closer and trying to deal. It was a stark, cold, long night. I returned to my hotel room at about 5 a.m. and waited for a reasonable time to call my boss and let him know that I would not be presenting that day, but would be traveling to Pittsburgh for the funeral later that afternoon.

Willy packed up the children and put them on a plane to

Pittsburgh. Tom R. flew in as well and the events were blurry and difficult. My brother, Sam, led the family meeting asking us all to contribute to the expenses and to clarify our roles. This set me off, and I was uncooperative and unable to feel part of the family in this moment. I was outspokenly put off by the business-like details and pouted. It made me angry, as I didn't want to play any role or pay any money. I just wanted to be in the grief I felt as his child. My father and I had not had the best couple of years before he passed. I went to Jacksonville on two occasions and tried to go out to eat with him or walk and talk alone, but those were disappointing visits. He had already distanced himself and drifted off and away when sitting in his favorite chair. I suppose he was cutting his attachments unconsciously. He was 93 years old and readying himself to let go. At his funeral and for a long time thereafter, I did not fully digest the loss. In December of that year, only one month after my father's death, I turned 50 years old and saw Tom R. for the last time at my birthday party. It had been quite a year.

In 2001, I decided to go out on my own into private practice as a special educator. Pine Ridge was deteriorating, the head of school was a poor leader and had replaced senior, more experienced employees with a batch of youngsters who had a weak grasp on the field of learning disabilities (LD). Like a rat leaving a sinking ship, it was time for me to go. To facilitate this gutsy move, I reached out to Zelda Zeleski, the Head of Special Education for The Chittenden South Supervisory Union with whom I had attended countless meetings during the previous four years. I needed a safety net and some guaranteed income while I built up my private practice. She offered me the entire contract servicing all LD students in the private schools in the district. Sweet – that was a 16 hour per week contract, which brought me into the halls of all private schools in my area: a coup. The opportunity to build relationships with teachers, administrators, guidance counselors, parents and heads of school in the four major private high schools virtually assured me of a pipeline of work for as long as I wanted to work. I renovated my outbuilding, set up shop, and named it LittleWing Learning Center after the Jimi Hendrix song LittleWing. This song has, to my ear, the finest Hendrix guitar solo ever played with a far-reaching and haunting riff, which my neighbor Scott played beautifully.

When I bought this property in 1997, I envisioned designing and opening my own business again with a yen to set and maintain my own standards. I had no idea what that might be, but the potential percolated until the right moment came along. Where both work and love are concerned, I often describe my timing and choices as opportunities that arise and I see them for just that. It is my job to live in readiness and recognize the fit when it shows up. Frankly, for me, photography has some of the same task of recognition at its core. When doing portraits or nature photography, something intangible presents itself to me as the light and an expression on a face or in a field merge and offer an unforgettable and ephemeral sight – Minor White's "Equivalence." In the deepest recesses of who I am, I was already looking for it and in a flash of recognition, I press the shutter with a steady touch. Minor White on the subject: *Equivalence is a function, an experience, not a thing. Any photograph, regardless of source, might function as an Equivalent to someone, sometime, someplace. If the individual viewer realizes that for him what he sees in a picture corresponds to something within himself – that is, the photograph mirrors something in himself – then his experience is some degree of Equivalence.*

It is so satisfying to have the world rise up to meet me and for me to say yes. All is right with the world and, when this happens, I experience a sense of belonging. As I age, I often sense that the conveyor belt has slowed down and wonder if my habit of recognition will continue to serve me as well as it has so far?

Earlier that year, my neighbor, Scott J., came over to ask permission to cut down a tree on the margin of our properties. I had a five-month-old puppy named Hendrix; Scott is a fine guitarist who played Stevie Ray Vaughn and Hendrix covers. He was 24 years my junior, but we had an inexplicable connection right away: some kind of past life zap rang out as he crossed in front of me on the conveyor belt. I recognized him as important and familiar to me in spite of our age difference. Scott and I had a romantic relationship for about four years on and off. He had had a punishing childhood, never knew his father, was abused by his alcoholic mother's male partners and shipped off to social services at about twelve years old. This second family had its own share of tragedies. I often said to Scott when he felt abandoned by his adopted family, "No, you didn't get the grand, ocean liner, The Queen Elizabeth, but you got a decent tugboat that pulled you out of an even worse situation. Be grateful!" As a really fine guitarist, Scott often skillfully played LittleWing with such exquisite lonely-hearted pitch, that I fell back in love with that tune all over again. When it came time to name my new venture, that was it: LittleWing. I visualize my work as putting little wings under students who struggle to learn, recognizing that I am a product of the 60s in which I came of age.

If I remember back to the medium's message in rural Florida some 20 years prior to meeting Scott, I would have to say that he is the "one I held." We had no intentions of staying together long-term as our age difference would become untenable to both of us, and Scott wanted children. We went about our relationship with this in mind and, as hard as it might seem to pull such a thing off, we did! When he relapsed a few times on my watch, we ended our romantic connection, but I was instrumental in encouraging him to become an electrician as he is meticulous and mechanical; I knew this would be a perfect career for him. He worked full-time and went to school at night, then apprenticed for many years in order to gain his Masters Electrician status. I stood by him in moments of exhaustion and doubt, and he stayed with it and supported me in many ways fixing this and that at home. He gives me way too much credit for his success, but it has earned me a lifetime friend. I cannot imagine my life without Scott. Likewise, he encouraged me to go out on my own, sung my praises, and gave me the support to take this risky professional step. As the years progressed, Scott married and now has a beautiful wife and son. I adore each of them: we are family. He remains one of my dearest friends. It is Scott who I can call at 3 a.m. if I have an emergency. And, if the medium from rural Florida is right, it will be Scott at my deathbed, hopefully some many years hence.

Once again, the subject of fate comes up for me as I am certain I would not have met Scott so easily out in the world. How is it that he lived next door with his brother, had a Hendrix connection, and that we shared an instant recognition of each other as people who would support our individual growth? I have encountered more than my good share of amazing people at just the right time in my life and it's uncanny how they have snuggled in under my skin and become family to me. Scott is one such angel.

Dr. Eggerman, a psychiatrist at the University of Pittsburgh, with his dapper suit and spectacles and my high school English teacher from Simmons College with her hair piled high and flowing skirts also showed up at crucial times in my adolescence. Things were really bad between my parents, and we children were suffering the consequences of living with parents caught up in their own abusive relationship. Perhaps Father Logue, the parish priest and my father's confident, or one of my sisters may have suggested that the twins needed to talk to a therapist. However the connection was made, I got to spend a glorious hour talking to Dr. Eggerman about what I experienced and how I felt. I was around ten or twelve years old at the time and this was the first time anyone took an interest in the content of my inner life. As he listened to me and took me seriously, I spread my wings and spoke about my various insights and theories. He was the first person who complimented me on my precocious understandings, indirectly confirming the gifts of the seventh child and joining me in the land of apples. This psychiatrist held my hands, looked me in the eye and said I was special and smart. He had me repeat those words and encouraged me to keep on dreaming and thinking. He told me I was exceptional; I carry his words with me. No doubt, he could also see my deep loneliness, trauma scars, and the other effects of living motherless in a tumultuous household.

A few years later, in high school, I met another rescue pilot, my 11th grade English teacher, Sandra Kauper. She recognized me as an excellent student in her class and told me so in the hours I spent in her office between the end of school and the beginning of gymnastics practice. I desperately needed these two angels, and they showed up. I called my high school to check my facts and learned that Sandra only taught at Upper St. Clair High School for one year before getting married and moving away. When the registrar sent me this message I looked her up in the yearbook and was delighted to see her face again. Ms. Kauper gave me an extra book list including: Dostoyevsky's *Crime and Punishment*, Henry James' *A Portrait of a Lady* and Ayn Rand's *Fountainhead*. For the first time in my life, I met people like me on the pages of these books. I was thrilled, less lonely and intellectually challenged by the predicaments certain characters encountered. These books changed my life and affirmed the value of an interior life, adventure, and the quest for truth. Fyodor Dostoyevsky said and I listened: *Above all, don't lie to yourself. The man who lies to himself and listens to his own lie comes to a point that he cannot distinguish the truth within him, or*

around him, and so loses all respect for himself and for others. And
having no respect he ceases to love.

Though I had been scribbling for years in my diaries, my dream to become a writer was hatched. This teacher lovingly spent extra time reading my reflections on these books and encouraging me to write imitations of style and extensions to the ideas that caught my attention. She took my intellect seriously just as Dr. Eggerman took my insights seriously. What terrific guides – thank you, wherever you are! Intellectually, this was exactly what I was hungry for, I stayed up late to read and write and marvel at how these characters connected truth with the capacity to love and, in Henry James' case, at his continuously looking at Isabel through her mind's eye as she developed from an adolescent girl into a wise woman. I could see her interior and listen to her inner dialogue and found a friend in Isabel as I too had lengthy dialogues with myself over this and that. Suddenly, I was observing characters outside of my sphere of experience. In observing Isabel, I could see how her husband, Gilbert Osmond, was a cad after her money long before she sees it; she had to come to terms with his duplicity, and her inner life is revealed along the way. I watched her wade in over her head and cringed. I saw her spirit tarnish with experiences of betrayal and then regain its shine with the steady development of responsibility in the service of her personal freedom and independence. Years later, with uncanny similarities, I would watch myself deal with my marriage in much the same way and for many of the same reasons. Like in *Crime and Punishment,* the importance of an adherence to truth in defining identity became my mantra, and I try to live by it still – *Sat Nam* – I am truth. Characters in books became my role models, they lived a larger-than-life existence and, not only did I live vicariously through them, but my idea of what it meant to live a rich life came from the influential characters in these novels. I also played Hendrix and Bob Dylan albums for hours in my bedroom and memorized the lyrics to over a dozen of my favorite Dylan songs. When I heard his tune *To Ramona*, a few years ago, I still knew every word. *Ramona come closer shed softly your watery eyes / The pangs of your sadness will pass as your senses will rise…*

Each of these inspirational musicians and writers valued and spoke from the perspective of people with a rich interior life, people who reflected and made art out of painful and joyful reflection. I wanted this for myself as I felt I belonged in their company more than I had ever belonged to anything or anybody. This connection further answered my questions about why I was different. I began to understand and believe that I had the sensibilities of an artist.

The effects of having not been seen as a youngster and even in my marriage have followed me around and manifested in different ways at different times. When I do get recognition, I roll around in it like a cat in the sun. An eagerness to be seen and loved, to offset the familiar ghost of loneliness, has perhaps brought me headlong into relationships with men who were not a good match for me. At this time in my life, I was able to observe the capacity to see and to love in these artists. My yearning to be seen and loved now had a name as I listened to how well Dylan knew Ramona and how well Henry James knew Isabel. I wanted to know and be known in that penetrating way. I longed for the quality I possessed and used in my observations of people to be turned toward me for once. My hiatus from wondering who I was and how I got to be that way transformed into a hunger to live whatever it was I had going on. A new courage arose in me as I could see myself in Isabel Archer or in Ayn Rand's celebration of the power and potential in the individual and their maps of how to develop and flourish.

Of course, I have since begun to see these heroines in a different light, but they served their purpose. They were nothing short of crowbars, wedging me out of Pittsburgh, Catholicism and the limitations I saw in most of the people around me. I used them to form an ideal of who I wanted to become, which got me out of the rut of spending energy analyzing what I didn't want to be. These writers and musicians were rescue pilots too.

For nearly twelve years, I have been with a man who feels little urgency to verbalize his feelings, neither to himself nor to others, though his interior brims with thoughts, ideas and puzzlements. His inner processes revolve less around people and feelings and more around spatial relationships, problem solving and devising methods. I remember our first date in June, 2007 at a restaurant called *Smokejacks,* a favorite of mine at the time – a good pick. He drove to my place in his black Audi, and we had our first drink on my deck. A designer/architect by profession, Dave B. wore wire rim glasses, Italian loafers with no socks, and a linen pin-striped shirt. I met him, then, in his citified design-architect persona and saw refinement in his ankles, bone structure, and thoughts. Looking back, I now see how that persona was making room for change as his long-standing dream to develop a farm and his farmer persona in Vermont was pushing up like a tulip in spring. Dave had recently purchased a house on ten acres in west Charlotte and had a few chickens scratching around the place along with his black and white Springer Spaniel named Shakespeare. As I was a 16th-century-English literature major with a focus on Shakespeare, there was promise there too, I thought. Years later, I learned his dog had been named after a fishing rod – gotta love the lesson on why not to interpret things too literally. In my Jamesian true innocence, I believed that things are as they seem to be. Today, he has 30 or so Icelandic sheep, three green houses, three llamas, 70-100 chickens, a Marema guard dog, a second house with ten acres and employs a manager, who runs the farm in his absence during the week. He commutes from New York to Vermont every weekend in his white Ford pickup truck.

Though not as inclined to share his interior as I had wished for when we met, I am privileged to see a more practical, spatial, mechanical, entrepreneurial mind at work, which is likewise interesting. I assumed that he too was living on a juicy draw from a complex interior that I might hear all about and, though maybe he is, it remains a silent, private place that I witness obliquely in his creations and actions. I have struggled with our differences from time to time: a tug and pull between logos and pathos, but there is a love force between us. Like the conceptual artist he is, he envisions and then builds chicken coops, sheep shelters, and farm stands, now sprinkling the fields and margins of his 20 acres. He can hold many acres in his mind's eye and then proceed to shape them with plantings and grazing meadows, with willow, hazelnut and black locust trees, with raised beds and greenhouses, with ponds and fences all in line with the high aesthetic qualities of building and landscape architecture.

Like mine, Dave's life hasn't been easy. He has lived through his parent's divorce, his own and the emotional disruptions they engendered. Everyone's life is hard somehow, but his recourse is to seal over his feeling center and escape through work. Over time, he has wandered deeper and deeper into farming and spends his time and energy servicing the responsibilities of animal husbandry, bee-keeping and farm chores when not in New York working intensively as a designer/architect: the quintessential Gemini.

For the most part, the silences and aloneness are worth it, because he is interesting, kind and talented, and he leaves me alone. Though I don't want to be left alone entirely, it is preferable to interference, and, alas, it's familiar. It has been a long-distance relationship, and the tenor and rhythm of the time we spend together is determined mostly by his double-profession schedule.

In the months before we met, Dave had bought his property in *my* town; we were introduced by mutual friends as he wanted to find a girlfriend. We traveled to London, New York City and Pittsburgh to see art. In the early years of the farm, we birthed lambs together in the barn in the middle of the night. Throughout the dozen years of our relationship, we have both retreated and reappeared emotionally. I want to be loved but not crowded or possessed by a man; my anxious style of attachment works well with Dave's avoidant and ambivalent style. The formality of this sonnet I wrote shows the tensions and seasons of a long term relationship; when we met, I had a hunch we would be together for a long time.

What Lies Below

A light and quiet glaze of snow
Covers sweet what lies below;
Beneath the top it heaves and burns
A twitch of heart I've come to know.
Might there be so soon a turn,
From rush of stream to creep and do
The things that fill a daily life
Like fix and plan and work and glue
The chair, the trip, the house, the strife.
Or do I wish to be his wife?
And wend my way from place to place
With hoe and rake and pot and knife
To lie beside him dressed in lace,
And hold in mind and heart his face,
And hold in mind and heart his face.

There is almost too much to say about the dynamics that brought us and keep us together and apart. As noted, he is a visionary and exceptionally talented, both loosely and tightly strung. We have changed with age, and though I can wax nostalgic about the early days, I feel committed to him and to us. He and I take breaks from each other and then reconnect with more insights and renewed desire to be together. Perhaps he represents a circuitous return to the Irish and I'm partly there in order to clean up some unfinished business of my own. I am at home by his side. T. S. Eliot captures this circling around and coming home pattern best: *We shall not cease from exploration, and the end of all our exploring will be to arrive where we started and know the place for the first time.*

More questions: maybe I have lost the capacity to throw myself in and willingly give up some territory of the self? Or maybe I have never picked an emotionally available man? Or maybe I need the kind of space this relationship offers me for whatever reasons? Regardless, I know the soft safety that opens me is still present when I am with Dave. I can imagine that the depth and complexity of my inner life is a mined field for the uninitiated. Dave may be lost in this terrain; his own interior remains a sweet blur to him and mine must be blinding and provocative all at once.

Besides, developing his farm along with animal husbandry skills revealed to me Dave's capacity to make management decisions unfamiliar to me. His lifestyle choice includes mercy killing, burying sick animals who die, or selling them if they are unfit to breed. This capacity dawned on me slowly, as I am tender-hearted and probably incapable of those kind of actions and decisions. Birthing baby lambs in the middle of the night is one thing, letting them go, digging graves and burying them is quite another. This character trait in Dave sometimes frightens me along with his emotional shifts and silences: his interior is likewise a mined field to me. My "Crow Blood" poem takes that fear to an exalted, fantastic place.

CROW BLOOD

A single drop of congealed blood
A red pearl, luminous in the chaos
of scissored blades of grass,
chartreuse and spiked.
Crows had been a problem
in need of a solution on the farm.
Kill and hang a menacing crow
on the fence, in the garden
to chase the bandits away…
the folk advice goes.

He decided he would use
his 22 rifle with silent bullets.
We practiced, me too,
and I hit close to the oatmeal can
on my first shot
knowing how to bring on the
required concentration and stillness –
I'm an old hand at that.

Dave shot it but the crow
whirled in a spastic show of pain.
Not completely dead yet.

Still, I can see the blood –
it stains me and holds me
like an after-image
from a camera's flash
lingering and disturbing.
I turn toward the porch
and watch as he hurries
to collect more bullets,
needed extras to finish the job.

I turn in the extravagant fear
that this could be my blood
as it has been extracted already
by a cold and uncivil hand
of a man unknown to himself
a man who can kill.

My theory of unfinished business is viable as the psyche has had a way of tricking me into fields of experience that are necessary in order to complete growth: the rules of karma. When I speak of fate, I am sometimes referring to this psychological and emotional pull toward unfinished business. Cleaning it up in therapy is one way to go, but falling in love is far more real. It also offers an opportunity to fall back in love with yourself, with the person you see in your lover's eyes. With this perspective in mind, I am grateful for the opportunity to heal the cracks left over from childhood rejections. It has been worth the ride if the outcome takes me beyond limitations I still live with unwittingly. Sometimes, even with the several long breaks, a certain readiness to return rises in both Dave and me. As Hamlet says: *the readiness is all.*

Everything works itself out. Elements of destiny, fate or free will coupled with the urge to move toward or away from an experience can be mysterious. *It* may be meant to happen now, or, if *it* is supposed to happen later then *it* won't happen now. *It* can be anything: love, work, friendship, writing, publishing, travel, etcetera. I live this truth in an active way, participating in a dynamic interaction of readiness and timing in order to recognize what is coming across the conveyor belt of life. Be prepared and then, when something happens to precipitate a change, you will have done the inner work to support the consequences. This is not unlike the concepts of perfect balance in martial arts – be ready to move in any direction at any time without preparation.

It is not lost on me that Dave is an emotionally unavailable man and not altogether an easy fit for me. As I was raised by an emotionally unavailable mother, being invisible is what I was and what I know how to be in relationship, but it is not what I want! Though I find comfort in my solitude, I also crave love. Stephen Dunn, in his remarkable poem, "A Postmortem Guide" gives direction to his eulogist in advance …*say that I loved / my companions most of all. / In all sincerity, say that they provided / a better way to be alone.*

As I have built my life brick by brick on a foundation of core aloneness – the distance in love may, on the other hand, be a good fit for me – even if therapists assure me I could change how I attach and relate to aloneness but, at this point, why? Marriage is one way to be in relationship, year-by-year choice is quite another, allowing for growth, breaks and reunions. It suits me!

Well into my 60s, I reflect on how many passionate relationships with men end in betrayals and divorce; I choose not to relive that pattern. It has been easy to be beside Dave as we understand each other in countless ways: we seek silence; we are self-made; we express ourselves through work; we are creative; we love great food and wine; we are introverts; we know how to walk beside the person we love...sometimes but not always. It is complicated; too much proximity makes me squirrelly, too little leaves me feeling unseen, and I can easily feel unseen and unimportant given my triggers. No doubt, I experience estrangement with Dave from time to time and we part ways for months and then rekindle. We value the many years of experiences we have shared: my children's graduations and his children's weddings. When I am alone in my house and garden, I see the many gifts Dave has given me: the water wheel, the thick linen swatches of fabric, the distressed green dry-sink, the red-concrete ball, and the glass table he made for my office: *objets d'art*. Of the many books he has given me, *The Wild Braid* by Stanley Kunitz meets me in the realm of erotic impulse and aesthetic receptivity. Like the poet Kunitz, moments of merging are critical to my well being and identity. In the Kunitz poem "Touch Me," the final refrain describes me: *Touch me, remind me who I am*. Dave loves me in his way, I have reason to believe in and trust what is between us.

A Plum Under the Stars

We went to his farm – Shakeyground
after our supper of risotto and salmon.
On the way, he queried me about
Asperger's and anxiety, then he snoozed
for the fifteen minute ride to our town
to forget if there might be relevance.
I understand avoidance, it's a friend –

He wakes up, smells the farm
feels the seize of brakes; he's a good car napper.
We start the close-up-chores at the farm stand.
I take in the tallow smell of sheep hides hanging over
rows of heirloom tomatoes and onions and zucchini
and next to the hanging art of garlic, wild dancing forms.
It's been a while…

Next we go in the house to change into boots –
it smells funny like juniper or some new cleaning product
and the dining room chairs are upside down on the table.
My feet are happy in the familiar slide of his too-big boots
I like wearing his clothes – having him on me –
We start toward Zita, the guard dog, and the chicken coop.
The dog gets fed and patted, half wild and splendid, she purrs.

On our way now to the coop, no flashlight only
starlight and moonlight and velvet darkness –
He wobbles to a stop – reaching and bending to
squeeze the plums – ahh, the perfect one for me.
He hands it to me and moves on – my feet click in the boots,
his phone flashlight comes on and dances across the fields,
I follow, woozy with the rush of soft, plum-flesh and tart skin.

I'm reminded of my friend Pam flirting with my brother Joe
one summer 50 years ago in a pool as she ate a dark plum
with a savvy and seductive play of her mouth on the plum –
I was still a baby in the world of sex, but I remember this still
as I hustle to keep up to his sway and the jumpy flashlight –
to keep up with the present, perfect deja vu night walk
under the stars, through the fields, behind my love.

The crickets scream, the moon lingers still as a god
illuminating us as gates clang and boots click and
the phone light bobs up and down all the way to the chickens.
They are all perched in rows, making humming sounds
in the chicken poop smell I hate while I love the scene,
the sound, the sight – we each take a photo of the chickens
his vertical, mine horizontal – close the latch –
metal on metal music.

Back in my sandals, back in the car,
we hope the dogs are okay…
Only a four minute drive to my house,
less dark, less messy, less magical
chaos becomes order, Memphis, Rumi and Roxy get out to pee
we head up to bed – I sleep against his back – it's hot –
the comforter slides off,
we lay in the moonlight in the buttery sheets
while the tape of the night and day plays softly in my mind
and slows and fades and rumbles me to sleep against him.
Good night to all that is – the man, the plum
and the music we make.

The concept of near enemies in Buddhism has to do with mistaking a counterfeit thing for the real thing. The most easily understood duo is compassion vs. pity. In spiritual terms, these near enemies are most often something you see in yourself as a growth point but, in fact, they are delusional roadblocks. Often when I question a relationship, I find myself rewinding time and asking why I didn't see this "thing" that is unhinging me before now? Surely I have missed some "red flags" early on in multiple relationships, or maybe a wasteland looks like a compelling wilderness. As I said earlier, perhaps the psyche tricks me into growth as when love comes in through the back door and takes me by surprise. Once I'm in…the work begins in earnest. Truth be told, I am not sure this isn't the ultimate purpose of love: mutual growth. I wonder with keen perplexity about this.

Fundamentally, it is also true that I don't believe in changing people, and I whole heartedly subscribe to the philosopher and poet John O'Donohue's words on the subject of solitude and an essential kind of personal wilderness: *Solitude as the sense of space is nourishing. What usually happens with solitude is that people equate it with loneliness, which frightens them. But I don't know anyone who has a good friendship or love relationship in which there are not long periods of solitude. There is a way in which we treat our relationships almost like a colonial expedition: we want to colonize the space, all the territory in between, until there is no wilderness left. Most couples who have deadened in each other's presence have colonized their space this way. They have domesticated each other beyond recognition. …I think it is more interesting to be with somebody who still has his or her wilderness territory….*

I have made myself that promise too because for me it is essential to be with someone who has some "wilderness territory." Consistent with the "near enemies" notion, it is easy to mistake navigable landscapes for impenetrable ones. Many times, I look at my drive toward languor and merging as my only gateway into sharing my interior, and maybe that's a burden to others. I try to take a clear-eyed look at my motivation to share and unite with another person as perhaps a gnawing, insatiable hunger. Or, maybe, because I know how to be self-sufficient and independent, I value and require this same independence in my man. I profoundly respect sweet companionship with another person at this point in my life, and it may well have grown paramount to all other aspects of romantic love. I must also confess to a realization that my work with the gifted population creates a precedent when it comes to patience and admiration for uniqueness in myself and in others.

Today, all of these influences converge in me and have become my friends in my tireless quest for beauty and truth. Because of them, I understand tradeoffs and consequences and accept the tenor and flavor of the fallout in my life using the perspective I honed from years with my nose in books and song lyrics. Study and sheer grit brought me to Europe and back, gave me courage to design and work in businesses where I could service my own high standards. The collage of my life opened in me a deep faith in the importance of education and self-transformation and confirms that belief with each passing year, each breath.

Since the Plato entries made by Mark Robson in my journal on Poets' Day, April 24, 2009, I have taken flight. My spirit has not been killed "whilst the body lives." I am a poet, the finest and most privileged of souls. I had the desire and the courage to become a mother and witness how the sheer joy of mothering has also healed the remaining cracks of my own motherless condition.

Each morning in winter, I get up at sunrise, throw a log on the fire, drink strong black coffee with my toast and bury my feet in the fur of my beloved dog, Rumi, who sits at my feet. Initially, the fire lights the darkness, and then the sun rises. In summer, I grow greens and flowers, perform work I love in a beautifully renovated space in a relatively safe, progressive state. My home is cottage-like, an old house that holds me day and night in all four seasons; it is adjacent to 200 acres, which I access freely. I have escaped my mother's shadow and still live with my father's spirit in the land of apples, and I am indeed the seventh child. My daughters are beautiful, successful women who work on human rights issues with verve, intelligence, and heart; they are my finest gift to the world. I believe I have carried the dangers and mysteries of the seventh child with care and dignity. It isn't always easy to be me, but I wouldn't change a dot on my map. My journey has followed the zigzag path of all those who ask the big question: "Who Am I?" and all those who try to live their way into the answer.